NOW
is the TIME...

...insights for living an
abundant life

NOW
is the TIME...

...insights for living an
abundant life

Christian
LIFE
A STRANG COMPANY

Most CHRISTIAN LIFE products are available at special quantity discounts for bulk purchase for sales promotions, premiums, fund-raising, and educational needs. For details, write Christian Life, 600 Rinehart Road, Lake Mary, Florida 32746, or telephone (407) 333-0600.

NOW is the TIME
Published by Christian Life
A Strang Company
600 Rinehart Road
Lake Mary, Florida 32746

www.charismahouse.com

Cover design by Whisner Design Group, Tulsa, Oklahoma

Copyright © 2008 by GRQ, Inc.
All rights reserved

ISBN 10:   1-59979-270-2
ISBN 13:   978-1-59979-270-5

BISAC Category: Religion/Christian Life/Inspirational

First Edition
08 09 10 11 12—9 8 7 6 5 4 3 2 1

Printed in the United States of America

To love is to will the good of another.
SAINT THOMAS AQUINAS

"Love the Lord your God with all your heart
and with all your soul and with all your
mind." This is the first and greatest
commandment. And the second is like it:
"Love your neighbor as yourself."

Matthew 22:37–39, NIV

NOW *is the* TIME...

Contents

Introduction 12

Make a Difference

1. Step Out in Faith 14
2. Move Beyond Fear 15
3. Go Within 16
4. Practice Success Strategies 17
5. Embrace Change 18
6. Dream Big 19
7. Move Toward Love 20
8. Cultivate Curiosity 21
9. Be Compassionate 22
10. Trust God's Timing 23
11. Turn Problems into Projects 26
12. See God in Others 27
13. Simplify Your Life 28
14. Admit Your Errors 29
15. Be Generous 30
16. Respect Yourself 31
17. Renew Your Vision 32
18. Be Appreciative 33

Renew Your Mind

19. Think Clearly 34
20. Spread Joy 35

21. Ask for Help 36
22. Live with Passion. 37
23. Make Small Changes. 38
24. Go with the Flow 39
25. Be a Better Friend 40
26. Play 41
27. Take a Class. 42
28. Start Anew. 43
29. Cultivate a Merry Heart 46
30. Be True to Yourself 47
31. Plant a Seed. 48
32. Read the Bible. 49
33. Share Love. 50
34. Pay Attention. 51
35. Speak Wisely 52
36. Serve Others 53

Build Your Character

37. Avoid Temptation 54
38. Work with Enthusiasm 55
39. Live Well 56
40. Cultivate Inner Stillness. 57
41. Be True to Yourself 58
42. Live with Honor 59
43. Extend Forgiveness 60
44. Embrace Mystery 61
45. Rest in Grace. 62
46. Start Your Day with Prayer 63
47. Celebrate Life 66
48. Age Gracefully. 67
49. Enjoy Small Pleasures 68
50. Go for a Walk 69

51. Do Your Best Work 70

52. Take Risks 71

53. Value Good Advice 72

54. Cultivate Character 73

Take the First Step

55. Be Courageous 74

56. Persevere 75

57. Cultivate Inner Power 76

58. Take Responsibility 77

59. Make a Decision 78

60. Take the Initiative 79

61. Be a Leader 80

62. Be a Servant Leader 81

63. Awaken the Genius Within 82

64. Cultivate New Ideas 83

65. Learn to Say No 86

66. Learn to Say Yes 87

67. Create Sacred Space 88

68. Teach Others 89

69. Travel 90

70. Contemplate Eternity 91

71. Live Life Passionately 92

72. Welcome the Dawn 93

Enjoy Life to Its Fullest

73. Live in the Present 94

74. Sleep in Peace 95

75. Live Artfully 96

76. Ask Questions 97

77. Trust Your Hunches 98

78. Be Authentic 99
79. Be Faithful in Small Things 100
80. Make Big Plans 101
81. Cultivate Wonder 102
82. Exercise Your Imagination 103
83. Be Silent 106
84. Know the Truth 107
85. Enjoy Music 108
86. Accentuate the Positive 109
87. Affirm Your Faith 110
88. Shed Bad Habits 111
89. Get Organized 112
90. Put Love into Action 113

Plan for Accomplishment

91. Release Worry 114
92. Make Time for Fun 115
93. Eliminate Distractions 116
94. Create Community 117
95. Choose Your Conversations 118
96. Listen Actively 119
97. Tithe Your Income 120
98. Ask for Guidance 121
99. Work Smarter 122
100. Think Long Term 123
101. See the Big Picture 126
102. Picture Success 127
103. Pace Yourself 128
104. Live Sustainably 129
105. Let God Handle It 130
106. Speak the Truth in Love 131

107. Find Common Ground 132
108. Walk Your Talk 133

Stretch Your Boundaries

109. Challenge Your Assumptions. 134
110. Count Your Blessings. 135
111. Seek Divine Wisdom. 136
112. Care for Your Soul. 137
113. Give Up Perfectionism. 138
114. Take a Sabbath. 139
115. Listen to Your Body. 140
116. Find Your Balance 141
117. Appreciate the Differences. 142
118. Be God's Ambassador 143
119. Invite Inspiration 146
120. Practice the Presence 147
121. Treasure This Moment 148
122. Work Playfully. 149
123. Cultivate Confidence. 150
124. Find Strength in Vulnerability. 151
125. Work Wholeheartedly 152
126. Attempt Great Things. 153

Go for the Good Life

127. Do What's Right for You. 154
128. Let Go of the Past. 155
129. Be Truly Free 156
130. Read a Good Book 157
131. Cultivate Contentment 158
132. Keep a Clear Conscience. 159
133. Value Humility. 160

134. Rule Your Mind............................. 161
135. Give Anonymously 162
136. Pray in All Situations....................... 163
137. Eliminate Nonessentials..................... 166
138. Expect the Unexpected 167
139. Trust in All Seasons........................ 168
140. Be Patient................................. 169
141. Be Productive.............................. 170
142. Be Hopeful................................ 171
143. Look for Role Models 172
144. Be Progressive 173

Live Successfully

145. Create Positive Change 174
146. Trust Your Finer Instincts 175
147. Enjoy Life 176
148. Keep Learning............................. 177
149. Recognize Opportunity 178
150. Be Cheerful 179
151. Seek Wise Counsel 180
152. Refrain from Anger 181
153. Be an Encourager.......................... 182
154. Depend on God............................ 183
155. Live in Peace 186
156. Remain Faithful............................ 187
157. Be Bold 188
158. Be Pure in Heart 189
159. Reach for the Stars......................... 190
160. Commit Your Future to God................. 191

NOW *is the* TIME...

Introduction

*Each of you must take responsibility
for doing the creative best you
can with your own life.*

Galatians 6:5, The Message

Your life is a gift from God, and how you live your life is your gift back to God. *Now Is the Time* offers simple reminders that life happens here, today, in the current moment. It encourages you to make the choices today that will enhance your life now and fulfill your God-given potential tomorrow.

This is the day that God has given you. Make the most of it, for now is the time to dream big, embrace change, exercise your imagination, step out in faith, and live life passionately. Know that you are always in the right place, at the right time, and doing the right thing when you make choices that are rooted in God's love and grace.

No matter where you go or what you do, you are in the center of God's grace. His love surrounds you and enfolds you and carries you through every circumstance. May these meditations be a reminder that you can choose to live freely in the light of God's love.

Now is the watchword of the wise.

Charles Haddon Spurgeon

To improve the golden moment of opportunity,
and catch the good that is within our
reach, is the great art of life.
SAMUEL JOHNSON

This is the day the LORD *has made;*
we will rejoice and be glad in it.

Psalm 118:24, NKJV

NOW
is the **TIME...**

To Step Out in Faith

When you walk, your steps will not be hampered;
when you run, you will not stumble.

Proverbs 4:12, NIV

*L*ike Moses and the Israelites crossing the Red Sea, it takes a step of faith to make the waters part. It takes courage to step out in faith. You may have no guarantees that things will work out; you have only your trust that God will carry you through. But God is faithful to those who dare to trust His promises, so today is a good day to be willing to step out into unknown territory in faith and trust. Simply move forward, assured tht God has you in His hands. You will see your faith rewarded in wonderful ways.

Faith is the substance of things hoped for,
the evidence of things not seen.

Hebrews 11:1, NKJV

The act of faith is more than a bare statement of belief,
it is a turning to the face of the living God.
CHRISTOPHER BRYANT

NOW
is the TIME...

To Move Beyond Fear

*Do not be afraid. Stand firm and you will see
the deliverance the LORD will bring you today.*

Exodus 14:13, NIV

*F*ear is something you learn. Caught up in mesmerizing stories of past failures and hurts, it is easy to talk yourself out of going for your dreams and doing what you know God is calling you to do. Identify the fear thoughts that are holding you back and replace them with thoughts of faith. Move beyond fear-based thinking and look at your life in the light of God's promises. You are larger than your fears, and God will help you move beyond the limitations of fear and doubt.

*Be strong and courageous! . . . For the LORD your
God will personally go ahead of you. He will
neither fail you nor abandon you.*

Deuteronomy 31:6, NLT

*Fears are educated into us, and can,
if we wish, be educated out.*

KARL MENNINGER

NOW
is the TIME...

To Go Within

What you're after is truth from the inside out.
Enter me, then; conceive a new, true life.

Psalm 51:6, THE MESSAGE

*T*he spiritual life begins in the heart. God works within the heart, in the quiet place where the true motives for all you do are revealed. Go within today and take time to be alone with God, listening to your heart and letting the Spirit tell you what you need to know. It is tempting to look at outer circumstances or the opinions of others, but it is the seed of quiet faith planted in the human heart that will grow into a transformed life. Once firmly pressed into your heart, faith will take root and grow steadily to fruition.

The kingdom of God is within you.

Luke 17:21, NIV

Prayer enlarges the heart until it is capable
of containing God's gift of himself.

MOTHER TERESA

NOW *is the* TIME...

To Practice Success Strategies

If the ax is dull and its edge unsharpened,
more strength is needed but skill will bring success.

Ecclesiastes 10:10, NIV

*I*f you want to be successful in life, you have to practice the strategies that lead to success. This begins with trusting God and asking for guidance. A positive attitude and a commitment to succeed are also essential to achieving real success. Look for ways to serve others and do what you do out of love, not fear. Study the examples of others and learn from their successes and failures. Hone your skills. Make your plans, do the work, and trust God to work all things together for good.

Commit your work to the LORD,
and your plans will be established.

Proverbs 16:3, ESV

Four steps to achievement. Plan purposefully. Prepare
prayerfully. Proceed positively. Pursue persistently.

WILLIAM ARTHUR WARD

NOW
is the TIME...
To Embrace Change

*The Lord—who is the Spirit—makes us more and more
like him as we are changed into his glorious image.*

2 Corinthians 3:18, NLT

*C*linging to the past is futile. Though you might crave the
comforts of what you already know, it is the nature of life
to grow, evolve, and change. Human beings grow through
the seasons of life, moving from childhood into adoles-
cence and then adulthood, from immaturity to maturity.
Embracing change does not mean throwing out valued tra-
ditions and relationships. Embracing change means that
you are open to God's bringing you fresh opportunities
and new possibilities. Choose a radical form of trust in
God today and welcome change into your life.

O LORD of hosts, blessed is the one who trusts in you!

Psalm 84:12, ESV

Change is the nursery of music, joy, life and eternity.
JOHN DONNE

NOW *is the* TIME...

To Dream Big

As the heavens are higher than the earth, so are My ways
higher than your ways and My thoughts than your thoughts.

Isaiah 55:9, NAS

Is your God too small? A big God is a God who inspires a larger vision of what life can be. So if you are willing to embrace a radical trust in God, then you can dare to dream big. Think about what you love to do and what you'd love to see happen. Consider the entire spectrum of your life in your immediate space and in the world. Think about your family, your work, your environment, your spiritual aspirations. Write those big dreams out in a notebook or journal. Now pray and ask God to show you how to make those dreams become reality. You may be surprised by how wonderful the answers will be.

Take delight in the LORD,
and he will give you your heart's desires.

Psalm 37:4, NLT

Never make the blunder of trying to forecast the
way God is going to answer your prayers.

OSWALD CHAMBERS

NOW *is the* TIME...

To Move Toward Love

Your steadfast love is before my eyes,
and I walk in your faithfulness.

Psalm 26:3, ESV

*G*od is love, and every step you take in the direction of love leads you straight to the heart of God. When you choose love instead of fear, you align yourself with the kingdom of God. Choosing to serve others in love is a reflection of how God loves you. Moving toward love also includes giving yourself permission to do what you love, to cultivate your gifts and talents to express love in the world. When faced with a choice today, ask yourself if you are motivated by love.

"Love the Lord your God with all your heart and with all
your soul and with all your mind." This is the first and
greatest commandment. And the second is like it:
"Love your neighbor as yourself."

Matthew 22:37–39, NIV

He who is filled with love is filled with God himself.
SAINT AUGUSTINE

NOW
is the TIME...

To Cultivate Curiosity

The heart of him who has
understanding seeks knowledge.

Proverbs 15:14, NKJV

*I*f you think you have all the answers, you don't even know what the questions are. Limited thinking means limited options. Learn to cultivate the quality of curiosity in your life. Instead of making snap judgments, be open to new ideas. Be observant and pay attention to the marvelous world that God created. George Washington Carver studied the humble peanut and discovered hundreds of uses that would serve humanity. Ask God to help you keep an open mind and let your curiosity lead you into new adventures.

The heavens are telling of the glory of God; and their
expanse is declaring the work of His hands.

Psalm 19:1, NAS

For lack of attention a thousand forms of
loveliness elude us every day.

EVELYN UNDERHILL

NOW
is the TIME...

To Be Compassionate

The LORD's lovingkindnesses indeed never cease,
for His compassions never fail. They are new
every morning; great is Your faithfulness.

Lamentations 3:22–23, NAS

*C*ompassion is an attribute of God's character and action toward you. As God has been compassionate and forgiving to you, so you can choose to cultivate compassion for others. Compassion offers a heartfelt awareness of the struggles and sufferings of others. While it is tempting to pass on the other side of the street when you see someone in pain, be willing to reach out to someone who is hurting today. To act compassionately is to be God's hands and heart in every situation you encounter.

Chosen by God for this new life of love, dress in the
wardrobe God picked out for you: compassion,
kindness, humility, quiet strength, discipline.

Colossians 3:12, THE MESSAGE

I would rather make mistakes in kindness and compassion
than work miracles in unkindness and hardness.

MOTHER TERESA

NOW *is the* TIME...

To Trust God's Timing

If we hope for what we do not see,
we wait for it with patience.

Romans 8:25, ESV

*T*iming is everything. Learning to trust divine timing is an art that requires patience and faith, but it bears blessed fruit. If you are experiencing delays or are frustrated because results don't come as quickly as you had hoped, take a moment to commit your hopes to God—then relinquish your need to control or predict when, where, and how things will unfold. God's timing is like the seasons, unfolding in a higher wisdom than the human mind can understand. Trust that fruition will come in perfect ways, in God's time.

My times are in Your hand.

Psalm 31:15, NAS

Simply wait upon him. So doing, we shall be directed,
supplied, protected, corrected, and rewarded.

VANCE HAVNER

NOW *is the* TIME...

TO

Invite Inspiration

·

Find Your Balance

·

Work Wholeheartedly

·

Take a Sabbath

·

Eliminate Distractions

·

Choose Your Conversations

·

Create Community

·

Be Authentic

·

Live Artfully

Love is a fruit in season at all times, and within the reach of every hand.

MOTHER TERESA

The fruit of the Spirit is love, joy, peace, patience, kindness, goodness, faithfulness, gentleness and self-control.

Galatians 5:22–23, NIV

NOW
is the TIME...

To Turn Problems into Projects

Jesus looked at them intently and said, "Humanly speaking, it is impossible. But with God everything is possible."

Matthew 19:26, NLT

*I*f you've been wrestling with a problem—finances, career, relationships, health—why not take a new view of it? Instead of seeing it as a problem with all the dead-end feelings of despair, helplessness, and frustration that are attached to the word *problem*, start calling it a project instead. A shift in definition can offer a shift in perspective. The word *project* suggests a process that leads to a positive outcome. A project is something you can work on and learn from. Ask God to help you see possibilities instead of impossibilities.

Courage! Take heart! GOD is here, right here, on his way to put things right.

Isaiah 35:4, THE MESSAGE

Any fact facing us is not as important as our attitude toward it, for that determines our success or failure.

NORMAN VINCENT PEALE

NOW
is the TIME...

To See God in Others

*If someone says, "I love God," and hates his brother, he is
a liar; for he who does not love his brother whom he has
seen, how can he love God whom he has not seen?*

1 John 4:20, NKJV

*A*ll kinds of exciting possibilities open up when you decide
to look for the image of God in other people. Instead of
thinking about their faults and foibles or judging them by
the standards of a critical society, you begin to see the
sacred spark within them. Instead of just taking others for
granted, you become aware that everyone is precious in
the sight of God. Open your eyes today and become aware
of the God-given uniqueness of every human being, the
untapped potential each person carries within.

*God created human beings in his own image. In the image of
God he created them; male and female he created them.*

Genesis 1:27, NLT

---

*In every human face is visible the
Face of faces veiled as in a riddle.*
NICHOLAS OF CUSA

NOW
is the TIME...

To Simplify Your Life

God is not a God of confusion but of peace.
1 Corinthians 14:33, NAS

*S*implicity cuts through the clutter and brings order and openness to your life. If you feel buried under too many obligations and too much stuff, start clearing the clutter today. Instead of trying to do too much, mark out dates in your calendar for quiet time alone with God. Buy less stuff so you have less stuff to take care of. Clear clutter on your desk or clean out a cupboard. Choose simplicity over chaos in one area, and it will eventually affect all areas of your life.

Why do you spend your money for that which is not bread,
and your labor for that which does not satisfy?

Isaiah 55:2, ESV

> *Finding a way to live the simple life today*
> *is man's most complicated task.*
>
> HENRY A. COURTNEY

NOW
is the TIME...

To Admit Your Errors

How can I know all the sins lurking in my heart? Cleanse me from these hidden faults. Keep your servant from deliberate sins! Don't let them control me.

Psalm 19:12–13, NLT

*I*f you're too busy defending past mistakes, you'll miss the opportunity that errors and misunderstandings offer. Mistakes, errors, and failures are often the fertile compost that helps you grow a better life. A toddler keeps getting up after falling because she's determined to learn to walk. She concentrates on where she's going, not where she's been. So you can learn from your errors and move beyond them. Ask for forgiveness if necessary, and don't waste energy in self-justification. Ask God to help you learn from mistakes and move on.

People who conceal their sins will not prosper, but if they confess and turn from them, they will receive mercy.

Proverbs 28:13, NLT

It is human to err;
it is devilish to remain willfully in error.
SAINT AUGUSTINE

NOW
is the TIME...

To Be Generous

The world of the generous gets larger and larger;
the world of the stingy gets smaller and smaller.

Proverbs 11:24, THE MESSAGE

A generous heart gives in many ways. While the first thing
you might think of is money, there are other important ways
of being generous. Sharing yourself with others, taking time
to give back with no strings attached, volunteering, and
being an encouraging person who applauds others' gifts and
talents are some practical ways to live generously. Choosing
generosity is an act of faith that overcomes a scarcity
mentality. Instead of being afraid that there is not enough,
being generous is a statement of trust in God's abundant
generosity.

God will generously provide all you need. Then you will always
have everything you need and plenty left over to share with others.

2 Corinthians 9:8, NLT

It is possible to give without loving,
but it is impossible to love without giving.

RICHARD BRAUNSTEIN

NOW
is the TIME...

To Respect Yourself

*I will give thanks to You, for I am fearfully and
wonderfully made; wonderful are Your works,
and my soul knows it very well.*

Psalm 139:14, NAS

God made you in His image. You are unique, and God loves
you. Respect that uniqueness, and trust that there is a reason
you were born in this time and place. Perhaps that reason is
something you will create, change, establish, or otherwise
influence. You have a gift to offer, even if you do not yet
know what that gift may be. Knowing that God loves you
and has called you to participate in His creative work frees
you to respect yourself. As you respect yourself, you are more
able to respect others. God puts a high value on you, so
respect yourself.

Do not neglect the gift that is in you.

1 Timothy 4:14, NKJV

Our gifts are given to reflect the God we serve.
ADELINE LIM

NOW *is the* TIME...

To Renew Your Vision

How lovely are Your dwelling places,
O LORD of hosts!

Psalm 84:1, NAS

*I*magine you are standing on a mountaintop with God, looking down over the hills and valleys of your life. What would that view look like? Are you spending too much time drudging over details and missing the vision of your life? Now is a good time to ask God to show you a larger vision for your life. Think about what you would like to experience in your life—the goals, the aspirations, and your heart's desire. Affirm your willingness to make that vision a reality with God's help.

My soul longs for You, indeed,
my spirit within me seeks You diligently.

Isaiah 26:9, NAS

> *Vision encompasses vast vistas outside the realm*
> *of the predictable, the safe, the expected.*
> CHARLES SWINDOLL

NOW
is the TIME...

To Be Appreciative

Rejoice always, pray without ceasing,
in everything give thanks.

1 Thessalonians 5:16–18, NKJV

*E*very day, make it a point to appreciate life. Look around and be aware of the wonder of God's creation, including the simple things you take for granted. Think about what it takes to deliver a single cup of coffee for your morning break: growers in a far-off country, importers and distributors, the store where you bought it, the person who brewed it. Appreciate the creative efforts and coordination it takes to help make life more pleasant. Now express your appreciation to others—and to God—for these gifts.

I come to your altar, O LORD, singing a song
of thanksgiving and telling of all your wonders.

Psalm 26:6–7, NLT

The world will never starve for want of wonders,
but for want of wonder.

G. K. CHESTERTON

NOW
is the TIME...
To Think Clearly

*Be transformed by the renewing of your mind. Then you
will be able to test and approve what God's will is—
his good, pleasing and perfect will.*

Romans 12:2, NIV

*I*f you can change your thoughts, you can transform your
life. If your thoughts continually stray to old pathways of
negativity, doubt, and worry, it's time to get them back on
the straight and narrow way. Now is the time to consciously choose better thoughts that help you improve
your life and see it from God's perspective. The next time
you start having a thought of scarcity, choose to focus on
God's abundance instead. Every time you find yourself
caught up in muddled thinking, stop. Choose better, more
helpful thoughts.

*Whatever is true, whatever is noble, whatever is right, whatever
is pure, whatever is lovely, whatever is admirable—if anything is
excellent or praiseworthy—think about such things.*

Philippians 4:8, NIV

---

*A great many people think they are thinking when
they are merely rearranging their prejudices.*

SIR WILLIAM JONES

NOW *is the* TIME...

To Spread Joy

The joy of the LORD is your strength.
Nehemiah 8:10, NIV

*J*oy is your birthright. When you watch a child or hold a baby, you can feel the joy that comes so easily and naturally from within. When you see the beauty and grandeur of nature—your wonder-filled world—you experience joy. While joy is often lost in the hustle and rush of life, it is always waiting to be rediscovered. God promises that joy can be found even in the midst of weeping. So find joy in God. When you cultivate inner joy, then you are able to share the strength of that joy with others. And joy shared is joy multiplied.

You have made known to me the path of life;
you will fill me with joy in your presence,
with eternal pleasures at your right hand.

Psalm 16:11, NIV

Joy is the holy fire that keeps our purpose
warm and our intelligence aglow.
HELEN KELLER

NOW *is the* TIME...

To Ask for Help

Everyone who asks receives, and the one who seeks finds,
and to the one who knocks it will be opened.

Matthew 7:8, ESV

*Y*ou have to learn to receive as well as give. Life is a two-way street, and there is no shame in asking for help when you need it. There are many avenues for grace to meet you, and one of them is through people helping one another. If you're always the one who gives but is never willing to receive help from others, you're denying yourself a great blessing and denying others the opportunity to share their blessings with you. It's God's delightful way of answering your prayers.

Ask, and you will receive, that your joy may be full.

John 16:24, ESV

The race of mankind would perish did they cease to aid each other.
We cannot exist without mutual help.

SIR WALTER SCOTT

NOW
is the TIME...

To Live with Passion

Let us also lay aside every weight, and sin which clings so closely, and let us run with endurance the race that is set before us.

Hebrews 12:1, ESV

*H*ave you ever seen a great athlete in action? You'll see that he is fired up by a passion for his sport. An artist has a passion for form and color. A musician has a passion for melody, harmony, and soul-stirring rhythm. A dancer trains for years to achieve the physical ability to express passion in a performance. Give yourself permission to be passionate about life—whether it is a glowing interest in art, sports, or business, or a passion for spiritual understanding. Authentic passion is an expression of praise to God.

Do you not know that in a race all the runners run, but only one receives the prize? So run that you may obtain it.

1 Corinthians 9:24, ESV

> *God never makes bloodless stoics.*
> *He never makes passionless saints.*
> OSWALD CHAMBERS

NOW
is the TIME...
To Make Small Changes

The steps of a man are established by the LORD,
and He delights in his way.

Psalm 37:23, NAS

*I*t doesn't take cataclysmic events to change the course of your life. You can do it one small change at a time. A decision to take an exercise class can eventually lead to a healthier, more lithe body. Learning a new skill can open doors to unexpected opportunities. A novel is written one page at a time. Make a small change today and ask God to help you stick faithfully to your choice. Then watch your life transform as old habits drop away and new habits develop.

If you look carefully into the perfect law that sets you free,
and if you do what it says and don't forget what you heard,
then God will bless you for doing it.

James 1:25, NLT

Never be afraid to trust an unknown
future to a known God.

CORRIE TEN BOOM

NOW
is the TIME...

To Go with the Flow

*I have directed you in the way of wisdom; I have led you in
upright paths. When you walk, your steps will not be
impeded; and if you run, you will not stumble.*

Proverbs 4:11–12, NAS

*T*here is a natural ebb and flow to life. You can't push a
river, and you can't hurry the seasons. Instead of strug-
gling and resisting what is, relax and trust God. Go with
the flow of events and allow the inner wisdom of God's
perfect timing to unfold in your life. You'll find that God
has a better way of orchestrating your life. Unexpected
encounters, delays that turn out to be blessings in dis-
guise, and surprising solutions to seemingly unsolvable
problems arise when you learn to go with the flow.

*You will walk in your way securely
and your foot will not stumble.*

Proverbs 3:23, NAS

---

*Trust the past to God's mercy, the present to
God's love and the future to God's providence.*

SAINT AUGUSTINE

NOW
is the TIME...

To Be a Better Friend

*Live in harmony with one another; be sympathetic,
love as brothers, be compassionate and humble.*

1 Peter 3:8, NIV

What kind of friend you are depends on what kind of person you are. You need to develop your inner life to create great friendships. See your friends through God's eyes. Love your friends as God loves you—with faith and forgiveness. Love your friends for who they are, and let them love you by sharing your true thoughts and feelings. Be honest with close friends. Put the social masks away. Let down your hair and show a trusted friend the real you. Then you'll be a better friend.

*Make a clean break with all cutting, backbiting, profane talk. Be
gentle with one another, sensitive. Forgive one another as quickly
and thoroughly as God in Christ forgave you.*

Ephesians 4:31–32, THE MESSAGE

---

*Treat your friends as you do your pictures,
and place them in their best light.*

JENNIE CHURCHILL

NOW
is the TIME...
To Play

Satisfy us in the morning with your unfailing love,
that we may sing for joy and be glad all our days.

Psalm 90:14, NIV

*I*f you've been too busy to play, you've been too busy. You were made in God's image and meant to play—not just when you were a child but also now as an adult. Play revitalizes the spirit and restores a sense of perspective. Scientists talk about the breakthroughs that come when they've taken time away from the laboratory to rest and play. When you relax and take a break, your mind relaxes and new insights flow. So be like a little child for a while, and take time off for play.

The true object of all human life is play.
G. K. CHESTERTON

NOW
is the TIME...

To Take a Class

Wisdom will come into your heart,
and knowledge will be pleasant to your soul.

Proverbs 2:10, ESV

*B*e an eager student of life. Just because you've graduated from school doesn't mean you stop learning. Learning is a lifelong process. Give yourself the gift of structured learning by taking a class. You could study medieval poetry or pottery or business or needle arts. From theories of physics to theology and biblical studies, there is a whole world of learning that can stimulate your thinking and expand your understanding. Increased knowledge enriches your understanding and helps you grow as a person.

Buy truth—don't sell it for love or money;
buy wisdom, buy education, buy insight.

Proverbs 23:23, THE MESSAGE

Learning is not attained by chance. It must be sought
for with ardor and attended to with diligence.
ABIGAIL ADAMS

NOW
is the TIME...

To Start Anew

Put on a heart of compassion, kindness, humility,
gentleness and patience; bearing with one another,
and forgiving each other.

Colossians 3:12–13, NAS

*E*ach day is a new beginning. Holding on to old ways of
thinking, grudges and resentments, and worn-out ideas is
self-defeating. Now is the time to choose a fresh start and
a new attitude. Start with an attitude of forgiveness for
anyone who has trespassed against you. And forgive yourself, asking God to help you make a fresh start today. Be
open to new ideas and new possibilities. Remember that
you've never been here before, because each day offers a
new adventure.

If you forgive men their trespasses, your
heavenly Father will also forgive you.

Matthew 6:14, NKJV

Don't let yesterday take up too much of today.
WILL ROGERS

NOW *is the* TIME...

TO

Be Faithful in Small Things

·

Make Big Plans

·

Live in the Present

·

Create Sacred Space

·

Awaken the Genius Within

·

Take the Initiative

·

Practice Success Strategies

·

Move Toward Love

·

Be Pure in Heart

We must make choices that enable us to fulfill the deepest capacities of our real selves.
THOMAS MERTON

*I have learned in whatever situation
I am to be content.*

Philippians 4:11, ESV

NOW
is the TIME...

To Cultivate a Merry Heart

A merry heart does good, like medicine,
but a broken spirit dries the bones.

Proverbs 17:22, NKJV

*I*f a merry heart does good like medicine, does a cranky attitude make you sick? Scientists now report that attitudes can actually make a difference in health. So for the sake of your heart and happiness, actively choose to cultivate a more open and joyous attitude toward life. Play with children, who know the secrets of wonder. Pet a puppy or stroke a cat, God's animal teachers. And take time out to laugh with friends for the sheer joy of living.

Our mouths were filled with laughter, our tongues with
songs of joy. Then it was said among the nations,
"The LORD has done great things for them."

Psalm 126:2, NIV

Laughter has been implanted in our soul
that the soul may sometime be refreshed.
SAINT JOHN CHRYSOSTOM

NOW *is the* TIME...

To Be True to Yourself

Blessed is the man who trusts in the LORD.
Jeremiah 17:7, ESV

*Y*ou are a beloved, unique child of God—one of a kind. God gave you special gifts and talents that you were born to share with the world. But often that vision of who you are is obscured by the wear and tear of everyday life. If you've been feeling a bit insignificant or unworthy, learn to see yourself as God sees you, and take your hopes and dreams seriously once again. Be true to your deepest self, and trust that God has a purpose for your life.

Nothing in all creation will ever be able to
separate us from the love of God.
Romans 8:39, NLT

Each of us is absolutely unique
and irreplaceable in the eyes of God.
MARGARET LANGSTAFF

NOW
is the TIME...

To Plant a Seed

He shall be like a tree planted by the rivers of water, that brings forth its fruit in its season, whose leaf also shall not wither; and whatever he does shall prosper.

Psalm 1:3, NKJV

A garden is great therapy. It grounds you in the realities of God's kingdom, which is abundant and filled with earthly joys as well as heavenly splendors. A garden is a picture of heaven on earth, with fruit and flowers and green growing things. Plant a seed, and be reminded that there is a power within the seed that mixes with the earth and elements to produce fruit and flower. Remember also that a power is within you, a power that grows and flowers to produce spiritual fruit as well.

The fruit of the Spirit is love, joy, peace, patience, kindness, goodness, faithfulness, gentleness and self-control.

Galatians 5:22–23, NIV

The kiss of the sun for pardon, the song of the birds for mirth, one is nearer God's heart in a garden than anywhere on earth.

DOROTHY F. GURNEY

NOW
is the TIME...

To Read the Bible

*The word of God is alive and powerful. It is sharper than
the sharpest two-edged sword, cutting between soul
and spirit, between joint and marrow. It exposes
our innermost thoughts and desires.*

Hebrews 4:12, NLT

*S*piritual reading is good. But the Bible is something very special. It has nurtured the spiritual lives of millions over the centuries. From the poetry of the Psalms to the parables of Jesus, it offers illuminating words and ideas that can transform your life. If you are new to reading the Bible, buy a study Bible in a modern translation. It will help you discover spiritual riches immediately. For those who know and love the Bible, commit more time to study. Meditate on its inner meaning for you.

*Every part of Scripture is God-breathed and useful one way
or another—showing us truth, exposing our rebellion,
correcting our mistakes, training us to live God's way.*

2 Timothy 3:16, THE MESSAGE

---

*The Bible is alive, it speaks to me;
it has hands, it lays hold on me.*
MARTIN LUTHER

NOW
is the TIME...

To Share Love

Anyone who holds on to life just as it is destroys that life.
But if you let it go, reckless in your love,
you'll have it forever, real and eternal.

John 12:25, THE MESSAGE

*L*ove shared is love multiplied. You'll discover that love grows exponentially when it is given away. No need to hoard it. Be generous and daring in your sharing. Your love for others reflects God's love in the world. You are God's hands and heart and voice to others. Offer encouraging words, a helping hand, a caring heart. Even when you have been hurt and are afraid to love, reach out and allow yourself to love again. Doing so will heal your heart even as it warms the hearts of others.

God so loved the world that He gave His only begotten
Son, that whoever believes in Him should
not perish but have everlasting life.

John 3:16, NKJV

Inasmuch as love grows in you so in you beauty grows.
SAINT AUGUSTINE

NOW
is the TIME...

To Pay Attention

*Awake, O sleeper, rise up from the dead,
and Christ will give you light.*

Ephesians 5:14, NLT

*W*ake up to the everyday miracle of life, and don't miss
the messages from God hidden in common things. Every
moment offers a wonderful opportunity to see God in the
details, and you can begin right here and now. Living lessons of abundance hide in the heart of a simple rose. Bugs
and bees and butterflies busy themselves in God's glorious
creation. A friend's smile lightens your day. The stars
remind you of the vastness of the universe. A cool glass of
water refreshes, an image of spiritual refreshment.

*What a wildly wonderful world, GOD! You made it all,
with Wisdom at your side, made earth overflow
with your wonderful creations.*

Psalm 104:24, THE MESSAGE

---

*No moment is trivial since each one contains a divine
kingdom and heavenly sustenance.*
JEAN-PIERRE DE CAUSSADE

NOW
is the TIME...

To Speak Wisely

Let your speech always be gracious, seasoned with salt, so that you may know how you ought to answer each person.

Colossians 4:6, ESV

*G*racious speech that offers only truth and healing will save you from a great deal of heartache. Not only will you avoid gossiping and backbiting, but your spirit will be nurtured in a positive atmosphere. If your thoughts are dark and negative, they will spill out into your speech. But if you are cultivating a mind centered in God and in the hopeful and the positive, your speech will reflect what is in your heart. Speak only truth. Reserve judgment. Then you will have no regrets about what you say.

Kind words are like honey—sweet to the soul and healthy for the body.

Proverbs 16:24, NLT

If you wouldn't write it and sign it, don't say it.

EARL WILSON

NOW *is the* TIME...

To Serve Others

*Take my yoke upon you and learn from me, for I am gentle
and humble in heart, and you will find rest for your souls.
For my yoke is easy and my burden is light.*

Matthew 11:29–30, NIV

*S*ervice to others is no burden. You are most Christlike
when you give yourself in a spirit of service. Authentic
service is a joyous response to the love that God has given
you. Because you have come to understand how rich you
are in the things of God, this service to others overflows
from a full heart. If you're feeling low, you'll discover that
lifting another's burden lightens your heart. Loving service
that comes from gladness, not guilt, is sweet to the soul
and multiplies in joy.

Serve one another in love.

Galatians 5:13, NIV

---

*An effort made for the happiness
of others lifts us above ourselves.*
LYDIA M. CHILD

NOW *is the* TIME...

To Avoid Temptation

Pursue righteous living, faithfulness, love, and peace. Enjoy the companionship of those who call on the Lord with pure hearts.

2 Timothy 2:22, NLT

*T*hat big brownie looks so scrumptious. But you know that a moment on the lips means forever on the hips. The temptation to gossip is so strong, because you know a juicy tidbit that would add to the story going round. But regret comes after you've opened your mouth—and often costs a friendship. Everyone is tempted. So be honest with yourself and ask God for help to walk away from temptation. You can choose healthier pleasures and happier ways of relating to others. You won't regret resisting temptation.

God is faithful, who will not allow you to be tempted beyond what you are able, but with the temptation will provide the way of escape also, so that you will be able to endure it.

1 Corinthians 10:13, NAS

Every temptation is great or small according as the man is.

JEREMY TAYLOR

NOW *is the* TIME...

To Work with Enthusiasm

*Whatever you do, work at it with all your heart,
as working for the Lord, not for men.*

Colossians 3:23, NIV

*I*f you can't do the work you love, choose to love the work you do. Yes, it can seem like an impossible task, finding enthusiasm for work that does not interest you. But perhaps you have not yet discovered the potential in the job in front of you. All work is God's work, if you are willing to see God in the details. Put your heart into your work and take pride in what you do. Cultivate an enthusiastic attitude and trust that God will eventually reward your diligence.

*Do you see a man skilled in his work? He will stand before
kings; he will not stand before obscure men.*

Proverbs 22:29, NAS

> *Work without a love relationship spells burnout.*
> LLOYD JOHN OGILVIE

NOW
is the TIME...

To Live Well

Receive my instruction, and not silver, and knowledge rather than choice gold; for wisdom is better than rubies, and all the things one may desire cannot be compared with her.

Proverbs 8:10–11, NKJV

*P*eople talk about the good life. But what is a good life, really? It's more than money or prestige, for those things pass away. To live well is an art. So be the artist of your own life and create a life you can enjoy. Be authentic and follow your heart, even when your head says another thing. Ask for wisdom from God to guide you. Choose what's best for you, and use your best gifts to make a positive contribution. A life well lived is a blessing to all.

If any of you lacks wisdom, let him ask of God, who gives to all generously and without reproach, and it will be given to him.

James 1:5, NAS

He has achieved success who has lived well, laughed often, and loved much.
BESSIE ANDERSON STANLEY

NOW *is the* TIME...

To Cultivate Inner Stillness

*Be still, and know that I am God; I will be exalted
among the nations, I will be exalted in the earth.*

Psalm 46:10, NIV

*T*ake time away to meditate, pray, and still the chatter in
your mind. Instead of listening to the noisy world around
you, seek silence so you can cultivate a still place within
and listen to God's voice instead. Make this a habit, and
you'll find that you can take the stillness with you. Then
you can tune in to the voice of the Spirit even in the midst
of chaos. For once you have tasted this inner stillness and
spaciousness, you'll never be satisfied with a crowded
noisy life again.

He leads me beside the still waters.

Psalm 23:2, NKJV

---

*God is the friend of silence. See how nature works—trees,
flowers, grass—grow in silence? The more we receive in
silent prayer, the more we can give in our active life.*

MOTHER TERESA

NOW *is the* TIME...

To Be True to Yourself

*With my whole heart I have sought You; oh,
let me not wander from Your commandments!*

Psalm 119:10, NKJV

*W*hat does it mean to be true to yourself? It is easy to dis-
count your dreams and compromise your principles when
you are feeling unimportant and unimpressive. Who are
you to think you can be great? But greatness is an inside job
that begins by tapping into the potential for greatness that
God placed within your heart. Nurture your inner potential
by honoring your dreams, keeping your promises to yourself,
and holding fast to your personal integrity. God has created
you and called you, so be faithful and true.

*We are God's workmanship, created in Christ Jesus to do good
works, which God prepared in advance for us to do.*

Ephesians 2:10, NIV

> *No man can produce great things who is
> not thoroughly sincere in dealing with himself.*
>
> JAMES RUSSELL LOWELL

NOW
is the TIME...

To Live with Honor

Be devoted to one another in brotherly love.
Honor one another above yourselves.

Romans 12:10, NIV

*B*eing true to yourself means you are willing to honor your highest ideals as well as your best dreams. Living with honor also means honoring others, treating people with integrity and kindness. You keep your word, even if others are casual about their commitments. You live your life as if it counts, even in the small things. When you honor yourself and others by your thoughts, choices, and actions, you honor God as well. Today is a good day to live with honor, trusting in God's grace to help you do so.

He who pursues righteousness and loyalty
finds life, righteousness and honor.

Proverbs 21:21, NAS

To me the highest thing, after God, is my honor.
LUDWIG VAN BEETHOVEN

NOW *is the* TIME...

To Extend Forgiveness

*Do not judge others, and you will not be judged. Do not
condemn others, or it will all come back against you.
Forgive others, and you will be forgiven.*

Luke 6:37, NLT

*F*orgiveness can be hard work. It isn't easy to forgive someone who has hurt you. But as God extends His grace to all,
so you are called to extend forgiveness to those who have
wronged you. Be compassionate, because everyone struggles and all fall short of their potential for greatness.
Forgiveness not only brings God's grace into a situation, it
heals you as well. Refusing to forgive is like drinking poi-
son and expecting the other person to die. Ask God to
help you do the difficult but essential work of forgiveness.

*If you have anything against someone, forgive—
only then will your heavenly Father be inclined
to also wipe your slate clean of sins.*

Mark 11:25, THE MESSAGE

---

*If we could read the secret history of our enemies we should find in
each man's life sorrow and suffering enough to disarm all hostility.*

HENRY WADSWORTH LONGFELLOW

NOW *is the* TIME...

To Embrace Mystery

*H*ave you ever watched the sun come up, or kissed a baby's
cheek and marveled at the wonder of new life? Have you
ever had questions that you could not answer but still
knew they were worth asking anyway? If yes, then you have
glimpsed the mystery. Life does not come with a set of
instructions or easy explanations. Life can be difficult, but
it is also beautiful. When you cultivate humility and wonder,
resting in the mystery of God, you are growing into the
complex spirituality of a childlike faith.

*Religion points to that area of human experience where in one way or
another a man comes upon mystery as a summons to pilgrimage.*

FREDERICK BUECHNER

NOW
is the TIME...

To Rest in Grace

*To each one of us grace has been
given as Christ apportioned it.*

Ephesians 4:7, NIV

*Y*ou'll find reminders of grace everywhere if you are attentive. You can see God's gifts of grace in the beauties of creation and in the marvelous variety of people and how they express their unique gifts. You'll encounter grace in the choice of forgiveness, the provision for today's needs, and the still, small voice of the Spirit speaking to your heart. Grace is a gift; a gift freely given by a loving God. Cultivate an awareness of the everyday signs of grace, knowing the truth of God's love for you.

*God is able to make all grace abound to you, so that
having all sufficiency in all things at all times,
you may abound in every good work.*

2 Corinthians 9:8, ESV

*Grace can never be possessed but can only
be received afresh again and again.*

RUDOLF BULTMANN

NOW
is the TIME...

To Start Your Day with Prayer

*Listen to my voice in the morning, LORD. Each morning
I bring my requests to you and wait expectantly.*

Psalm 5:3, NLT

*B*efore the busyness of another day rushes in, start your day
with prayer. In the freshness of a new day you can go to God
with a rested mind and a heart clear of all distractions.
When you pray before you begin your day, you tune your
soul to God. Try praying before you get out of bed, while
you brush your teeth or take a shower, or as you get dressed.
Take a minute to sit quietly with God. Then your day
reflects the inner harmony of that secret morning time of
prayer. Pray for guidance, pray for others, and know that
God will show you He is with you all through the day.

*I, O LORD, cry to you; in the morning
my prayer comes before you.*

Psalm 88:13, ESV

*The entire day receives order and discipline when it acquires unity.
This unity must be sought and found in morning prayer.
The morning prayer determines the day.*

DIETRICH BONHOEFFER

NOW *is the* TIME...

TO

Be Generous

·

Turn Problems into Projects

·

Be True to Yourself

·

Pay Attention

·

Cultivate Curiosity

·

Work with Enthusiasm

·

Speak Wisely

·

Rest in Grace

·

Start Your Day with Prayer

*Always be in a state of expectancy
and see that you leave room for
God to come in as He likes.*

OSWALD CHAMBERS

The eyes of all look expectantly to You.

Psalm 145:15, NKJV

NOW *is the* TIME...

To Celebrate Life

Rejoice in the Lord always. I will say it again: Rejoice!
Philippians 4:4, NIV

*L*ife is a feast, so don't miss a single course. God's gifts are to be enjoyed, and even common days can be celebrations of life. Take today, for instance. What can you do to celebrate life right now? Give someone the gift of life by giving a flower, by offering your time and attention, or by lending a helping hand. Sharing the good things of life with someone else is always a cause for celebration. Make it a point to find something to celebrate today. Thank God for the gift of life.

Be glad in the LORD and rejoice, you righteous ones;
and shout for joy, all you who are upright in heart.

Psalm 32:11, NAS

You are to gather up the joys and sorrows, the struggles,
the beauty, love, dreams, and hopes of every hour
that they may be consecrated at the altar of daily life.
MACRINA WIEDERKEHR

NOW
is the TIME...

To Age Gracefully

The righteous flourish like the palm tree and grow like a
cedar in Lebanon. They are planted in the house of
the LORD. *. . . They still bear fruit in old age.*

Psalm 92:12–14, ESV

*I*n a society that worships youth, people are often afraid of
aging. But aging can be experienced gracefully, and the
years sit lightly on those who live in God's grace as they
grow older. Cultivate grace in all seasons and changes of
life. Aging is natural and inevitable. So instead of fighting
your age, count the blessings of growing older. Think
beyond the ageism and clichéd thinking of society. Make
a creative choice to reinvent what growing older means to
you. Cultivate a zest for life to feel forever young.

Gray hair is a crown of glory; it is gained in a righteous life.

Proverbs 16:31, ESV

Do not regret growing older. It is a privilege denied to many.
AUTHOR UNKNOWN

NOW _is the_ TIME...

To Enjoy Small Pleasures

Search high and low, scan skies and land, you'll
find nothing and no one quite like GOD.

Psalm 89:6, THE MESSAGE

_G_od is in the details, and daily life is made up of the details. Small pleasures are gifts of God that grease the wheels of life, refreshing you and reminding you of life's abundance. Small pleasures say, "Pay attention." Life is a sacrament, and everything is a gift from God. That cup of coffee, that flower, that delicious dinner, and that time with a friend— all are reminders of the wonders of creation. Remember that the miraculous often hides in the commonplace. Give yourself permission to enjoy a small pleasure today.

Light-seeds are planted in the souls of God's people,
joy-seeds are planted in good heart-soil.

Psalm 97:11, THE MESSAGE

It isn't the big pleasures that count the most:
it's making a great deal out of the little ones.

JEAN WEBSTER

NOW *is the* TIME...

To Go for a Walk

Let all the inhabitants of the world stand in awe
of Him. For He spoke, and it was done;
He commanded, and it stood fast.

Psalm 33:8–9, NAS

*W*alking calms both body and mind. Whether you walk
in the woods or down a city street, walking gets you away
from the desk and daily grind; it gives you new images to
contemplate. Let the rhythm of walking help you sort your
thoughts and process the day's events. God gave you two
legs, so get out and enjoy some invigorating exercise.
Walking lifts the spirits and tunes the body. Walk with a
sense of being in harmony with God's creation. Walk with
a sense of wonder, awe, and gratitude.

Let us walk in the light of the LORD.

Isaiah 2:5, NAS

If you are seeking creative ideas, go out walking.
Angels whisper to a man when he goes for a walk.

RAYMOND INMO

NOW *is the* TIME...

To Do Your Best Work

Make it your goal to live a quiet life, minding your own business and working with your hands.

1 Thessalonians 4:11, NLT

*I*n God's kingdom, even the most mundane work can be blessed service. Take pride in giving your best, knowing that you work for God and not for human beings. See all work as sacred and your job as more than just work; see your job as ministry. Bring more love to what you do. Do your work in the right spirit. See your career as a vocation, a calling from God. Do your best work, and trust God to take you to the next level tomorrow because you did your best work today.

Serve the LORD with gladness;
come before His presence with singing.

Psalm 100:2, NKJV

The shop, the barn, the scullery, and the smithy become temples when men and women do all to the glory of God!
CHARLES HADDON SPURGEON

NOW
is the TIME...

To Take Risks

*If the LORD delights in a man's way, he makes his
steps firm; though he stumble, he will not fall,
for the LORD upholds him with his hand.*

Psalm 37:23–24, NIV

*T*rue failure occurs only if you give up. The nature of risk
is that failure—or seeming failure—is one of the options.
But success is also one of the options. Whatever the outcome of taking a risk, you'll learn something new and
valuable. Second-guessing, trying to control outcomes, or
playing it safe can be deadening to the spirit. Take risks,
and trust God. Go ahead and do something you want to
do but are afraid to try. See this as a grand new adventure,
with God as your friend and companion along the way.

*Trust in the LORD forever, for the LORD,
the LORD, is the Rock eternal.*

Isaiah 26:4, NIV

---

*One can never consent to creep when
one feels an impulse to soar.*
HELEN KELLER

NOW *is the* TIME...

To Value Good Advice

Wisdom is with those who receive counsel.
Proverbs 13:10, NAS

*A*dvice is a two-way street. Good advice has a sense of give-and-take, as if the one advising is just as willing to hear your advice in return. Listen to the advice you hear, weigh and measure it, and then make your own decision. If you advise others, back up your advice with wise living and walk your talk. Know when to pay attention to advice and when to trust your own instincts. Ask God for discernment, both in taking and in giving advice. He will direct you in the way you should go, whether yea or nay. Pray for guidance, value advice, and then choose.

NOW *is the* TIME...

To Cultivate Character

*Blessed are those who hunger and thirst for
righteousness, for they shall be satisfied.*

Matthew 5:6, ESV

*C*haracter counts. Who you are speaks louder than words. When you choose to cultivate godly character in quiet trust, you are choosing to build your life on a solid foundation. As you learn to value strength of character in yourself, you will also begin to appreciate the qualities of courage, honesty, kindness, and moral strength in others. Knowing that God rewards character, even when others do not see or appreciate, is like knowing you have investments and money in the bank, even if you live modestly and simply.

*GOD, who gets invited to dinner at your place? How do we get
on your guest list? "Walk straight, act right, tell the truth."*

Psalm 15:1-2, THE MESSAGE

> *If I take care of my character,
> my reputation will take care of itself.*
> DWIGHT L. MOODY

NOW *is the* TIME...

To Be Courageous

The fear of the LORD leads to life,
so that one may sleep satisfied.

Proverbs 19:23, NAS

*T*he Cowardly Lion in the *Wizard of Oz* discovered that even when he was trembling and afraid, he had the courage to join his friends to rescue Dorothy from the Wicked Witch of the West. Courage often comes quietly, sneaking in through the back door instead of storming the castle gates. Real courage is a gift from God that helps even the most timid souls overcome their fears. When you are trembling in your boots, ask God to give you the courage to face and overcome your fears.

Because of Christ and our faith in him, we can now
come boldly and confidently into God's presence.

Ephesians 3:12, NLT

Bravery is the capacity to perform properly
even when scared half to death.

OMAR BRADLEY

NOW
is the TIME...

To Persevere

*Don't interfere with good people's lives; don't try to get
the best of them. No matter how many times you trip
them up, God-loyal people don't stay down long.*

Proverbs 24:15–16, THE MESSAGE

*Y*ou may have seen the poster showing a bewildered kitten
dangling on a branch, with the slogan beneath reading:
"Hang in there, baby." Sometimes that's a picture of how
life feels. But God doesn't leave you dangling in midair,
feeling helpless as a kitten. His unseen hand is there, holding you and helping you. Knowing that God gives you
every resource you need when you need it, you can be
tenacious and persistent, persevering even in those times
when you feel you're out on a limb. So never give up.

No one can snatch them out of my Father's hand.

John 10:29, NIV

> *Let me tell you the secret that has led me to my
> goal. My strength lies solely in my tenacity.*
>
> LOUIS PASTEUR

NOW *is the* TIME...

To Cultivate Inner Power

I pray that out of his glorious riches he may strengthen you with power through his Spirit in your inner being.

Ephesians 3:16, NIV

*T*he current age worships outward power, from armies and weapons that shock and awe to presidential offices and corporate suites where powerful men make decisions that change the course of history. But history is littered with the stories of empires once mighty that are now ended. True power is cultivated within: the power of compassion, wisdom, character, and love. Put your trust in the power of God and cultivate the spiritual power within, then you will experience an authentic power that changes hearts as well as lives.

Be strong in the Lord and in his mighty power.

Ephesians 6:10, NLT

When a man has no strength, if he leans on God, he becomes powerful.

DWIGHT L. MOODY

NOW
is the TIME...

To Take Responsibility

Everyone to whom much is given,
from him much will be required.

Luke 12:48, NKJV

You can choose to take responsibility not only for your actions but also for your thoughts. God gave you the gift of free will and the ability to reason. Remember that God promises you His strength in every situation. You have access to God's help, and that means you can make choices for the highest and best, because His help is always with you. Decide today that you will choose consciously instead of allowing old habits to rule you. Take responsibility for your choices, and trust God with the final results.

Choose for yourselves this day whom you will serve....
As for me and my house, we will serve the LORD.

Joshua 24:15, NKJV

I attribute my success to this: I never gave or took an excuse.
FLORENCE NIGHTINGALE

NOW
is the TIME...

To Make a Decision

The Spirit of truth... will guide you into all truth.
John 16:13, NIV

*W*hen making a decision of minor importance, it's advantageous to weigh the pros and cons, then make the best choice you can. In more vital matters, it is important to do more than just weigh the outward circumstances. Your decision must come from your inner spiritual wisdom and the guidance of God. In every decision you make, no matter how large or small, you are making a statement about what matters to you. So seek God's wisdom, then make decisions because they are right, not merely because they are convenient.

I will instruct you and teach you
in the way you should go.

Psalm 32:8, NKJV

We make our decisions, and then our
decisions turn around and make us.

F. W. BOREHAM

NOW
is the TIME...

To Take the Initiative

*Everyone then who hears these words of mine and does them
will be like a wise man who built his house on the rock.*

Matthew 7:24, ESV

*I*nitiative is doing the right thing without being ordered to
do it. You have to step up, step out, and get involved if you
want to have an impact on life. Weigh your options, ask
God for wisdom, and then take the first step. Do what you
can with what you have, and be willing to take the initiative
by doing the task that is in front of you, whether that task
is self-appointed because of a need you see or requested
because of a need others feel you are particularly suited to
tackle. By taking the initiative instead of waiting for someone else, you create the change you want to see in your life.

*If anyone loves me, he will keep my word, and my
Father will love him, and we will come to him
and make our home with him.*

John 14:23, ESV

---

*Nothing could be done at all if a man waited till he could
do it so well that no one could find fault with it.*

JOHN HENRY NEWMAN

NOW
is the TIME...

To Be a Leader

Do your best to present yourself to God as one approved, a worker who has no need to be ashamed, rightly handling the word of truth.

2 Timothy 2:15, ESV

*T*here are many kinds of leaders. Some are natural-born leaders. Others have learned how to be leaders when leadership was needed and no one else would lead. Whether you have a natural talent for leading others or you just see a task that must be done or a problem that must be addressed, now is the time when your willingness and skills are most needed. Your life up until this moment has been preparation for your future following God's call. When God calls you to step out and be a leader, obey that call, trusting that He will help you and guide you.

Go, and I, even I, will be with your mouth,
and teach you what you are to say.

Exodus 4:12, NAS

The growth and development of people
is the highest calling of leadership.
HARVEY S. FIRESTONE

NOW *is the* TIME...

To Be a Servant Leader

With good will render service,
as to the Lord, and not to men.

Ephesians 6:7, NAS

*S*elfless service is joyous service. True leadership reflects the kind of priorities that Jesus Christ lived by. He led by love and compassion, caring for others and serving the will of God. He described Himself as the Good Shepherd, who was willing to lay down His life for the sheep. You, too, can find joy and fulfillment in being a servant leader. Look for the latent potential and worth in those you work with, and think of ways to bring out the best in every person. Try to see others through God's eyes. See their worth, and serve them as God would have you do. You are God's heart and hands.

Whoever wants to be great must become a servant.

Matthew 20:26, THE MESSAGE

The true measure of a man is not the number of servants
he has, but the number of people he serves.

ARNOLD H. GLASGOW

NOW
is the TIME...

To Awaken the Genius Within

Your hands made me and fashioned me; give me understanding,
that I may learn Your commandments.

Psalm 119:73, NAS

*D*oes the word *genius* make you think of great intellectual achievers in science, music, and art, achievers like Albert Einstein, Mozart, and Leonardo da Vinci? You do not have to be a prodigy to be a unique person with God-given talents that can create good for others. You may have a genius for cooking or creating a thriving business or teaching children. Your childhood dreams, hopes, and talents were hints from God, and where you are now is the place to cultivate the special genius within—your unique gift to offer the world.

Know that the LORD Himself is God; it is He
who has made us, and not we ourselves.

Psalm 100:3, NAS

The life each of us lives is the life within the limits of our
own thinking. To have life more abundant, we must
think in limitless terms of abundance.

THOMAS DREIER

NOW *is the* TIME...

To Cultivate New Ideas

*Make me to know your ways, O LORD; teach me your
paths. Lead me in your truth and teach me.*

Psalm 25:4–5, ESV

*G*od gave you an original mind, if you are willing to use
it. So many people settle for hand-me-down ideas that no
longer fit today's circumstances. You may have a limited
idea of yourself or what is possible. But new ideas can
transform a world—whether it is the new product that cre-
ates a market or the new concept that frees an individual.
You have a limitless God who has created you to be a limitless thinker. Cultivate that gift by being open to new
ideas and possibilities.

*Commit your way to the LORD,
trust also in Him, and He will do it.*

Psalm 37:5, NAS

---

*Neither man nor nation can
exist without a good idea.*

FYODOR DOSTOYEVSKY

NOW *is the* TIME...

TO

Ask for Guidance

•

Release Worry

•

Do Your Best Work

•

Take Risks

•

Be a Servant Leader

•

Live Life Passionately

•

Cultivate New Ideas

•

Contemplate Eternity

•

Exercise Your Imagination

*Be ready at all times for the gifts of God,
and always for new ones.*
MEISTER ECKEHART

*God has given us different gifts for
doing certain things well.*

Romans 12:6, NLT

NOW
is the TIME...

To Learn to Say No

Let your "Yes" be "Yes," and your "No," "No."
Matthew 5:37, NIV

*D*o not be afraid to say no to that which does not serve your highest purposes. Even good things can be distractions from the calling and purposes of God for your life. A calm, solid "No" or "No, thank you" maintains much-needed boundaries and helps you focus on what is most essential. If you've been stretched thin and need time to rest, say no to those extra obligations. Know and respect your limits. Trust God to provide for the needs of others even when you cannot.

My people will live in a peaceful habitation, and in
secure dwellings and in undisturbed resting places.

Isaiah 32:18, NAS

Yes and No are the two most important words that you will ever say.
These are the two words that determine your destiny in life.

AUTHOR UNKNOWN

NOW *is the* TIME...

To Learn to Say Yes

A dream fulfilled is a tree of life.
Proverbs 13:12, NLT

*A*s you learn to say no to that which does not serve or support your highest good, learn also to say yes to what you most truly love and desire. These deep longings are God's whispers to your heart, and even if they need development and refinement, they must have your full commitment to come to fruition. Do not be afraid to say yes even when saying yes feels dangerous and daring. Yes opens the door to a new attitude and a new challenge. Yes begins discovery. If you have an urge to say yes to a new adventure, trust God to guide you.

Whatever your hand finds to do, do it with all your might.
Ecclesiastes 9:10, NIV

> *To say yes, you have to sweat and roll up your sleeves*
> *and plunge both hands into life up to the elbows.*
> JEAN ANOUILH

NOW
is the TIME...

To Create Sacred Space

Let me live forever in your sanctuary,
safe beneath the shelter of your wings!

Psalm 61:4, NLT

*T*hough God is everywhere, and therefore all places have the potential to be sacred, it helps to set aside a special room or corner for contemplation and renewal. It may be a quiet place in your home, a sheltered space in a garden, a tiny altar lit by candles on your dresser, or a favorite chair by the window. Let that be the place where you tryst with God to contemplate His love or to confide your troubles to His comforting care. This space will nurture you.

He who dwells in the secret place of the Most High
shall abide under the shadow of the Almighty.

Psalm 91:1, NKJV

These four walls provide a safe place from which I can contemplate
all sorts of possibilities, knowing that on my inner
compass, true north will always point me home.

LINDA WELTNER

NOW
is the TIME...

To Teach Others

Instruct and direct one another using good common sense.
...Let every detail in your lives...be done in the
name of the Master, Jesus, thanking God
the Father every step of the way.

Colossians 3:16–17, THE MESSAGE

You do not need a degree or a tenured position to teach others. All you need is a heart that cares and a skill to share. You can volunteer to teach children, offer to teach an adult education class, or open your home or studio or workshop to teach others the skills and craftsmanship you have spent a lifetime learning. But most important of all, you teach by example, wherever you go and whoever's life you touch. Recognize that you are the book of God that others are reading.

The teaching of your word gives light,
so even the simple can understand.

Psalm 119:130, NLT

A teacher affects eternity, he can never
tell where his influence stops.

HENRY ADAMS

NOW
is the TIME...
To Travel

I will meditate on the glorious splendor of Your majesty, and on Your wondrous works.

Psalm 145:5, NKJV

*T*ravel broadens the mind and leads you to new experiences. While you are seeing new places and faces, you are also expanding your inner understanding. Travel is as much a state of mind as it is a destination. Whether you take a trip to an exotic locale or just ramble down an unexplored street in your hometown, open your mind to new experiences and your heart to divine appointments with other people who are different from you. Such travel is another way to love God with your entire being.

I will meditate on Your wonders.

Psalm 119:27, NAS

Lord, make me see thy glory in every place.

MICHELANGELO

NOW
is the TIME...

To Contemplate Eternity

*His kingdom is an eternal kingdom; his dominion
endures from generation to generation.*

Daniel 4:3, NIV

*A*re you feeling overwhelmed? It is easy to be sucked into
false urgencies, whether by screaming headlines or an
overwhelming list of things that must be done before the
end of the day. In such times it is even more important to
go away to a quiet place and listen to whispers of eternity.
God will meet you there and teach you to have a larger perspective on life. You will find grace, peace, and wisdom
to keep you balanced when the urgencies of life would
unbalance you.

*We fix our eyes not on what is seen, but on what is unseen.
For what is seen is temporary, but what is unseen is eternal.*

2 Corinthians 4:18, NIV

*The few little years we spend on earth are only the first
scene in a Divine Drama that extends into Eternity.*

EDWIN MARKHAM

NOW *is the* TIME...

To Live Life Passionately

I will praise You, O LORD, with my whole heart;
I will tell of all Your marvelous works.

Psalm 9:1, NKJV

*S*ome people seem to face life with an armed neutrality; that is, they are afraid to enjoy life, disdainful of passion, and unwilling to risk their hearts on anything or anyone. This is not living; it's a vegetative state. You are made for better things. God gave you a heart to love, senses to explore and enjoy the world, and a high calling to make a difference wherever you go. As long as you are deeply rooted in God's love, you need never be afraid to express and enjoy your passion for life.

Blessed are those who keep His testimonies,
who seek Him with the whole heart!

Psalm 119:2, NKJV

I have seen life as it really is—ravishingly, ecstatically, madly beautiful,
and filled to overflowing with a wild joy, and a value unspeakable.

MARY PRESCOTT MONTAGUE

NOW
is the TIME...

To Welcome the Dawn

*I will sing of Your power; yes, I will sing
aloud of Your mercy in the morning.*

Psalm 59:16, NKJV

*G*ood morning! Are you ready to welcome the dawn? The peach-rose light is stealing over the hill ahead of the sun, and a new day is beginning. Whether you are an early bird who welcomes a sunny dawn or a sleepyhead who wants to cuddle under the covers on a cloudy day, each new dawn is God's gift to you. Welcome the dawn, and thank God for the opportunity to live another day. Offer a simple prayer of thanksgiving and a request for guidance, for God made this day.

*Let me hear of your unfailing love each morning, for I am
trusting you. Show me where to walk, for I give myself to you.*

Psalm 143:8, NLT

*Greet each day with your eyes open to beauty, your
mind open to change, and your heart open to love.*

PAULA FINN

NOW
is the TIME...

To Live in the Present

*I will bless You while I live; I will lift
up my hands in Your name.*

Psalm 63:4, NKJV

Yesterday is history. Tomorrow is a mystery. Today is a gift from God, and that's why it's called the present. The present comes moment by moment. Few people ever live fully in the present. They are forever anticipating what is to come or remembering what has gone. Decide that today you will fully savor each moment while it is here. You will be mindful of each moment the day brings and will embrace whatever comes. Embrace the moment, and you will find God is present with you always.

*Oh, let me sing to GOD all my life long,
sing hymns to my God as long as I live!*

Psalm 104:33, THE MESSAGE

When shall we live if not now?
M. F. K. FISHER

NOW
is the TIME...

To Sleep in Peace

In peace I will both lie down and sleep; for you alone,
O LORD, make me dwell in safety.

Psalm 4:8, ESV

*T*hank God for sleep! It's a good thing to be able to lay your head on the pillow and sleep. Even when you cannot sleep, thank God that you live to lie awake. You can hear God's still, small voice when the rest of the world is asleep. Listen in quiet anticipation. Let the peace of your night's rest depend on God's provision and protection. A good night's sleep will bring perspective in the morning. It is a good time to release all your concerns and relax into God's love and care.

If you lie down, you will not be afraid; when
you lie down, your sleep will be sweet.

Proverbs 3:24, ESV

Oh, how great peace and quietness would he possess who should
cut off all vain anxiety and place all his confidence in God.

THOMAS À KEMPIS

NOW *is the* TIME...

To Live Artfully

May the favor of the Lord our God rest upon us; establish the
work of our hands for us—yes, establish the work of our hands.

Psalm 90:17, NIV

*T*he Germans have a word for it: *Lebenskünstler*. It means
"life artist" and is an image of one who lives and appreci-
ates life itself as an art form. Artful living means making
the most of life itself, crafting it into an experience of
blessing for all. From savoring a delicious meal to enjoying
beauty and social graces, you can approach your life as the
canvas upon which you paint meaning and blessing. God
is the ultimate artist, and you are made in the image of
God. So enjoy life artfully!

Give unto the LORD the glory due to His name;
worship the LORD in the beauty of holiness.

Psalm 29:2, NKJV

There is not one blade of grass, there is no color in
this world that is not intended to make us rejoice.

JOHN CALVIN

NOW *is the* TIME...

To Ask Questions

GOD met me more than halfway,
he freed me from my anxious fears.

Psalm 34:4, THE MESSAGE

*G*od is not afraid of your doubts and questions. There is
no stupid question in eternity's classroom. There are only
people who are unwilling to disturb their own complacen-
cies. Now is the time to ask questions. It's how you learn.
Don't limit yourself to the small repertoire of what you
think you know. In a world as vast and mysterious as this,
the smart thing to do is to open your mind. You may not
find easy answers, but you will learn if you are willing to
ask questions.

I will put my hope in God! I will praise
him again—my Savior and my God!

Psalm 42:11, NLT

The first key to wisdom is assiduous and frequent questioning. For by
doubting we come to inquiry, and by inquiry we arrive at truth.

PETER ABÉLARD

NOW
is the TIME...

To Trust Your Hunches

*Tune your ears to the world of Wisdom; set your heart
on a life of Understanding....Before you know it...
you'll have come upon the Knowledge of God.*

Proverbs 2:2, 5, THE MESSAGE

*S*ome people have a more developed sense of intuition than others. Talk to a successful businessman, and you will often hear about making decisions on gut feelings or hunches coupled with experience and research. Whether negotiating a deal, navigating the stock market, or assessing the trustworthiness of a potential partnership, allow room for intuition to partner with the known facts. Ask God to help you discern the truth, and then trust that your spiritual radar is working to guide you in each situation.

*Those who are wise will find a time
and a way to do what is right.*

Ecclesiastes 8:5, NLT

*Knowledge is happiness, because to have knowledge—broad, deep
knowledge—is to know true ends from false, and lofty things from low.*

HELEN KELLER

NOW
is the TIME...

To Be Authentic

Let us draw near to God with a sincere heart in full
assurance of faith, having our hearts sprinkled
to cleanse us from a guilty conscience.

Hebrews 10:22, NIV

*Y*ou sell yourself short when you deny your inner truth to mollify other people. If you are being inauthentic, sooner or later other people will know. Life behind a mask is lonely, reducing you to being less than the person God created you to be. But when you choose to be true to your own convictions, you'll find that something inside you expands and opens up. You'll never satisfy everyone's expectations, but as long as you are walking in integrity and alignment with God, the authentic you will shine through.

The goal of our instruction is love from a pure heart
and a good conscience and a sincere faith.

1 Timothy 1:5, NAS

> *This above all: to thine own self be true, and it must follow,*
> *as the night the day, thou canst not then be false to any man.*
> WILLIAM SHAKESPEARE

NOW
is the TIME...

To Be Faithful in Small Things

If you're honest in small things,
you'll be honest in big things.

Luke 16:10, THE MESSAGE

*T*he returns you experience today reflect the effort you have put into realizing your goals. Skimping on the details will show in the final product. Be faithful in the small things, and God will bless and prosper your work. A fine crafts-man puts integrity into every detail of his work, and it shows. Do whatever it takes to make something right. So lay a strong foundation by paying attention to details and adhering to the fundamentals. Then you'll take pride in the work you do.

You have been faithful in handling this small amount,
so now I will give you many more responsibilities.

Matthew 25:21, NLT

> *Many people fail simply because they conclude that*
> *fundamentals simply do not apply in their case.*
>
> M. L. CICHON

NOW *is the* TIME...

To Make Big Plans

The heart of man plans his way,
but the LORD establishes his steps.

Proverbs 16:9, ESV

*I*t never hurts to make big plans. If God is your partner, then anything is possible. You can always scale back big plans, but small plans are often too shortsighted to take all possibilities into consideration. Think long term of ways to bless and prosper many people. Even the most expansive goal is reached one step at a time, so there is always plenty of opportunity for course adjustment. When you dare to dream big and make plans to match, you create room for the possibility of something wonderful to unfold.

The plans of the diligent lead surely to abundance.

Proverbs 21:5, ESV

To live is to change, and to be perfect is to change often.
JOHN HENRY NEWMAN

NOW *is the* TIME...

To Cultivate Wonder

O LORD, you are my God; I will exalt you; I will praise your name, for you have done wonderful things.

Isaiah 25:1, ESV

*J*esus recommended that His followers become like little children. A child is delighted and awed by the simplest of things: a puff of dandelion seeds, the mysterious workings of a car wash, the fascinating squishiness of mud puddles. You can cultivate a childlike sense of wonder. Become aware of the simple wonders of common things you might otherwise pass over. Wonder is a window on eternity, showing you that God, the Creator, has a surprise package for you to open every day if you have eyes to see.

Truly I say to you, unless you . . . become like children, you will not enter the kingdom of heaven.

Matthew 18:3, NAS

The dignity of the artist lies in his duty of keeping awake the sense of wonder in the world.

G. K. CHESTERTON

NOW
is the TIME...

To Exercise Your Imagination

*Open my eyes so I can see what you
show me of your miracle-wonders.*

Psalm 119:18, THE MESSAGE

*A*nother positive attribute of childhood that adults can consciously cultivate is using the imagination. A child pretends to be a ballerina or an astronaut, dreaming of future potential. You can exercise the God-given gift of imagination to find creative solutions. Use your imagination to explore career options or solve problems. Better yet, take time to play imaginatively, tapping into the part of you that is intimately connected to God. Paint something wonderful on the screen of your imagination, and then ask God to help you make it reality.

*O LORD, our Lord, how majestic
is your name in all the earth!*

Psalm 8:9, NIV

---

*Man's imaginative inventions must originate with God and
must in consequence reflect something of eternal truth.*

J. R. R. TOLKIEN

NOW
is the **TIME...**

TO

Picture Success

•

See the Big Picture

•

Value Good Advice

•

Live Sustainably

•

Let God Handle It

•

Enjoy Small Pleasures

•

Age Gracefully

•

Speak the Truth in Love

•

Challenge Your Assumptions

How you spend your time is more important
than how you spend your money.
Money mistakes can be corrected,
but time is gone forever.
DAVID B. NORRIS

Those who are wise will find a time
and a way to do what is right.

Ecclesiastes 8:5, NLT

NOW
is the TIME...

To Be Silent

I've cultivated a quiet heart. Like a baby content in its mother's arms, my soul is a baby content.

Psalm 131:2, THE MESSAGE

*C*lose the door on the chatter. Turn off the music and the media. Enter your prayer closet and taste the sweetness of silence. Intimacy with God deepens when words are left behind. It's just you and God, alone together, in silent communion. Take long walks in nature, allowing silence to sink in as you wander in God's creation. When you make time for silence, you are making time for a deeper spiritual dimension in your life. Then you can go back into the world, carrying that inner silence with you.

Righteousness will bring peace. Yes, it will bring quietness and confidence forever.

Isaiah 32:17, NLT

Sinking again into silence, the truth of words bears us down into the silence of God.

THOMAS MERTON

NOW *is the* TIME...

To Know the Truth

"Let each one of you speak truth with his neighbor,"
for we are members of one another.

Ephesians 4:25, NKJV

*Y*ou may believe certain facts about yourself. You tell your-self you're too fat, too skinny, too young, too old, too broke, too uneducated. The list of negatives can be end-less. You can easily see a problem and diagnose a disease. But that is seeing from a limited perspective. In God's kingdom, facts are not the truth. Facts change, but God's truth is eternal. From God's perspective, all those limiting facts are not who you really are. Know this important truth: you are a spiritually magnificent child of an unlimited and loving God.

The sum of Your word is truth, and every one of
Your righteous ordinances is everlasting.

Psalm 119:160, NAS

Lord, grant me weak eyes for things that are of no
account and strong eyes for all the truth.
SØREN KIERKEGAARD

NOW
is the TIME...

To Enjoy Music

Praise the LORD, for the LORD is good;
celebrate his lovely name with music.

Psalm 135:3, NLT

*M*usic reflects the ordered nature of creation, and listening to music can tune you in to the higher harmonics of God's hidden glory. From the mathematical precision of a Bach fugue to the lush romanticism of Beethoven, from the sacred sounds of choral music to the upbeat rhythms of pop and rock, music is an expression of energy and mood. Spend a few minutes today listening to music that you love. The sacred geometry of rhythm and the higher harmonic of melody can lead you to a place of deeper joy and devotion.

Sing to God, sing praises to his name.

Psalm 68:4, ESV

> *The aim and final reason of all music should be nothing else*
> *but the Glory of God and the refreshment of the spirit.*
> JOHANN SEBASTIAN BACH

NOW *is the* TIME...

To Accentuate the Positive

To him who is able to do immeasurably more than all we ask or imagine, according to his power that is at work within us, to him be glory.

Ephesians 3:20–21, NIV

*I*s your glass half empty or half full? Are you concentrating on what's wrong and what you lack? Or are you looking at the good that is already available to you and trusting in God's grace—a grace that can work all things together for good even when it seems that everything is getting worse? Plant a tiny seed of faith by accentuating the positive in your thoughts and conversation. This is an active faith that is willing to believe in God as source and provider, grateful for every blessing.

If you had faith like a mustard seed, you would say to this mulberry tree, "Be uprooted and be planted in the sea"; and it would obey you.

Luke 17:6, NAS

I learned really to practice mustard seed faith, and positive thinking, and remarkable things happened.

SIR JOHN WALTON

NOW
is the TIME...

To Affirm Your Faith

*You can pray for anything, and if you
have faith, you will receive it.*

Matthew 21:22, NLT

*S*ome days it is easier to have faith than others. It is good
to affirm your faith on any day, but especially valuable to
affirm faith on a day when doubts cloud your mind. Take
a moment to write down an affirmation of faith. Put it on
an index card and carry it with you in your pocket or
purse. It might be a personal affirmation, such as "I am
guided by God." Or it may be a positive scripture, such as
"God is love." Or it could be an affirmative statement, or
a quotation that encourages you right now, such as "You
can do it."

*God did not give us a spirit of timidity, but a
spirit of power, of love and of self-discipline.*

2 Timothy 1:7, NIV

---

*Even in the life of a Christian, faith rises and
falls like the tides of an invisible sea.*

FLANNERY O'CONNOR

NOW
is the TIME...

To Shed Bad Habits

We demolish arguments and every pretension that sets itself up against the knowledge of God, and we take captive every thought to make it obedient to Christ.

2 Corinthians 10:5, NIV

*H*uman beings are creatures of habit. Sometimes those habits are not favorable, and that's the time to ask God for help in changing them. Instead of focusing on getting rid of a bad habit, think about cultivating a positive habit in its place. Human beings respond more naturally to rewards than to punishment. Cultivate a better habit, and in the process you will naturally begin to shed the old bad habit. Ask God to show you one habit that needs to be changed, and what helpful habit can replace it.

Let the words of my mouth and the meditation of my heart be acceptable in Your sight, O LORD, my strength and my Redeemer.

Psalm 19:14, NKJV

A nail is driven out by another nail.
Habit is overcome by habit.
DESIDERIUS ERASMUS

NOW
is the TIME...

To Get Organized

God is not a God of confusion but of peace.
1 Corinthians 14:33, ESV

*Y*our desk is piled high with unopened mail, and the in-box is overflowing with things to take care of. No matter where you look, there's a distracting pile of stuff. It's time to get organized. As you clean and organize your surroundings, you'll find that your mind feels organized as well. Creating harmony and order is worth every bit of effort because it will make life run more smoothly. You'll not only feel a sense of accomplishment, but your spirit will be soothed. God is with you in mess or order, but doesn't order feel better?

Harmony is as refreshing as the dew from Mount Hermon that falls on the mountains of Zion. And there the LORD has pronounced his blessing, even life everlasting.

Psalm 133:3, NLT

Good order is the foundation of all good things.
EDMUND BURKE

NOW *is the* TIME...

To Put Love into Action

Faith, hope, and love abide, these three;
but the greatest of these is love.

1 Corinthians 13:13, ESV

*I*t's good to say you love someone. But love isn't fully expressed until it's put into action. Take a moment to pray about ways you could put love into action in your own life. Make a list of five or six specific actions you could take to demonstrate love practically. Now choose one action and do it. Take the garbage out. Offer to cook dinner tonight. Call or send a card to let someone know you're praying for him or her. Tackle the fix-it project you've been putting off. Pick up the shirts at the laundry. One act of kindness offers tangible evidence of love.

Let us not love with word or with tongue,
but in deed and truth.

1 John 3:18, NAS

> *Love seeks one thing only: the good of the one loved. It leaves*
> *all other secondary effects to take care of themselves.*
>
> THOMAS MERTON

NOW *is the* TIME...

To Release Worry

Worry weighs a person down; an encouraging
word cheers a person up.

Proverbs 12:25, NLT

*W*orry is like negative prayer. The more your mind plays imaginary movies of dire scenarios or magnifies the problems you face, the less energy you have for truly addressing and solving the issues. Focus all that worry energy on something more constructive. If there is something you can do toward solving the problem, figure out what it is and then do it. If there is nothing you can do right now, then give your worries to God. Your problem is in safe hands. Demonstrate your trust in God by going on with your day. Release worry, and let God handle it.

Do not worry about tomorrow; for tomorrow will care
for itself. Each day has enough trouble of its own.

Matthew 6:34, NAS

Fear and worry are interest paid in advance
on something you may never own.

AUTHOR UNKNOWN

NOW
is the TIME...

To Make Time for Fun

As the days of a tree, so will be the days of my people; my chosen ones will long enjoy the works of their hands.

Isaiah 65:22, NIV

*F*un is good medicine and food for the soul. It lifts your spirits. It refreshes your outlook on life. Scientists now say fun has even been proven to enhance health. So what are you waiting for? Give yourself the gift of a playdate. Don't worry. God will be with you in your enjoyment. Human beings are the ones who confuse spirituality with workaholism. A truly spiritual person can balance play and work, lighthearted fun and serious business. When God created the feast of life, He included fun on the menu, too.

It is useless for you to work so hard from early morning until late at night, anxiously working for food to eat; for God gives rest to his loved ones.

Psalm 127:2, NLT

The real joy of life is in its play. Play is anything we do for the joy and love of doing it, apart from any profit, compulsion, or sense of duty.

WALTER RAUSCHENBUSCH

NOW
is the TIME...

To Eliminate Distractions

Be still before the LORD and wait patiently for him.
Psalm 37:7, NIV

There are many potential distractions in a 24-7 modern world. There is always a cell phone to answer, e-mails to check, or some other distraction to tempt you. Whether you have a job to do or a desire to spend time alone with God, eliminate distractions by focusing on one thing at a time. Turn off the cell phone. Check e-mails only twice a day. Put up a Do Not Disturb sign and close the door. You'll work more efficiently and have better concentration for prayer by eliminating distractions.

Hear me as I pray, O LORD. Be merciful and answer me!
Psalm 27:7, NLT

Through a spiritual discipline we prevent the world from filling our lives to such an extent that there is no place left to listen.

HENRI NOUWEN

NOW
is the TIME...

To Create Community

*If we walk in the Light as He Himself is in the
Light, we have fellowship with one another.*
1 John 1:7, NAS

*F*or those who seek to live the spiritual life, it is essential to
balance private devotion with the companionship of like-
minded people who are also seeking to grow spiritually. If
you are not already involved with a church or spiritual
community, ask God to guide you to a group of people
who can share the journey, giving you roots that support
and sustain, and encouraging you to spread your wings
and fly. Make a commitment to participate regularly in
meaningful community that serves the highest good of all.

*You are no longer foreigners and aliens, but fellow citizens
with God's people and members of God's household.*

Ephesians 2:19, NIV

---

*Unless we give part of ourselves away, unless we can live with
other people and understand them and help them, we are
missing the most essential part of our own lives.*

HAROLD TAYLOR

NOW
is the TIME...

To Choose Your Conversations

The mouth of the righteous is a well of life.
Proverbs 10:11, NKJV

*C*hoosing your conversations goes beyond merely avoiding gossip or negative talk, to choosing your friends and the people you spend your time around. As you grow in the spiritual life, you'll find you have less interest in the complaint sessions or trivial subjects that once seemed so absorbing. You'll want to choose your conversations carefully as you hone in on what really matters to you. Spend time in conversations that inspire and motivate you instead of wasting energy on trivialities.

The wise of heart is called discerning,
and sweetness of speech increases persuasiveness.
Proverbs 16:21, ESV

Our words are a faithful index of the state of our souls.
SAINT FRANCIS DE SALES

NOW
is the TIME...

To Listen Actively

Oh yes, he's our God, and we're the people he pastures, the flock he feeds. Drop everything and listen, listen as he speaks.

Psalm 95:7, THE MESSAGE

*L*istening is one of the greatest gifts you can give to another human being. Active listening means that you will respond to what another is saying with focused attention. You might want to paraphrase and repeat back what was said for greater clarity and understanding. You can do this with another human being. You can also do this with God. Pick a scripture to meditate on, and let God speak to you through it. Turn it into a personal prayer. Then be silent and actively listen for God's wisdom.

Listen, my son, and be wise,
and direct your heart in the way.

Proverbs 23:19, NAS

One of the best ways to demonstrate
God's love is to listen to people.
BRUCE LARSON

NOW
is the TIME...

To Tithe Your Income

"Bring the whole tithe into the storehouse, that there may be food in my house. Test me in this," says the LORD Almighty, "and see if I will not throw open the floodgates of heaven and pour out so much blessing that you will not have room enough for it."

Malachi 3:10, NIV

*T*ithing is another way to become more active in your spiritual life. Giving 10 percent of your income is one way to commit to a regular and sustained practice of giving back to God. Begin with what is comfortable for you. Take a portion of the income you have received and give it to that which spiritually nourishes and blesses you and others. Give to your church or a worthy cause, or even give to an individual who has inspired and encouraged you. Tithing opens the doors to even greater blessing and prosperity.

Of all that You give me I will surely give a tenth to You.

Genesis 28:22, NAS

There is nothing wrong with people possessing riches. The wrong comes when riches possess people.
BILLY GRAHAM

NOW *is the* TIME...

To Ask for Guidance

You are my rock and my fortress; therefore,
for Your name's sake, lead me and guide me.

Psalm 31:3, NKJV

Never feel ashamed to ask God for guidance. Life is complex, and there are so many unknown factors that affect outcomes and events. You are not alone, and God is more eager to guide you and give you wisdom than you can ever imagine. Even when you think you've messed things up with poor decisions or wrong attitudes, God is always ready to meet you where you are. With God as your guide and source, anything is possible. So ask for guidance today, and then follow through on it.

Guide me in your truth and teach me, for you are God
my Savior, and my hope is in you all day long.

Psalm 25:5, NIV

I know not the way God leads me,
but well do I know my Guide.

MARTIN LUTHER

NOW
is the TIME...

To Work Smarter

*Pay careful attention to your own work, for then you will
get the satisfaction of a job well done, and you won't
need to compare yourself to anyone else.*

Galatians 6:4, NLT

*T*here is a hidden grace in work. Grace, a gift from God, is
found within the act of doing a job or offering a service. It
is unveiled in those self-forgetful moments when you are
absorbed in the work itself. It may start with a job that
must be done, but soon the labor itself becomes an act of
love. Instead of working just for money, work smarter.
Bring love to your work, whatever the job may be. You'll
discover God's blessing waiting for you in the work, no
matter what you do.

*Go to work in the morning and stick to it until evening without
watching the clock. You never know from moment to
moment how your work will turn out in the end.*

Ecclesiastes 11:6, THE MESSAGE

*No one else can tell you what your life's work is, but it's important that
you find it. There is a part of you that knows—affirm that part.*

WILLIS W. HARMAN

NOW
is the TIME...

To Think Long Term

*Look at those who are honest and good, for a
wonderful future awaits those who love peace.*

Psalm 37:37, NLT

*I*t's a short-term world, with stock values measured by
quarterly returns and the latest hit or best seller becoming
the measure of a successful career. But today's headlines
wrap tomorrow's garbage. So when you're making plans,
dare to dream larger dreams. Like the workers who crafted
the medieval cathedrals, work on something beautiful that
will outlive you. Whether you are making practical finan-
cial decisions or planning a better future, invest in choices
favoring lasting returns that will bring blessing to many
generations. Ask God for wisdom in long-term planning.

*Oh, how sweet the light of day, and how wonderful to
live in the sunshine! Even if you live a long time,
don't take a single day for granted.*

Ecclesiastes 11:7–8, THE MESSAGE

---

*A rock pile ceases to be a rock pile the moment a single man
contemplates it, bearing within him the image of the cathedral.*

ANTOINE DE SAINT-EXUPÉRY

NOW *is the* **TIME...**

TO

Celebrate Life

•

Share Love

•

Trust God's Timing

•

Renew Your Vision

•

Spread Joy

•

Live with Passion

•

See God in Others

•

Be True to Yourself

•

Cultivate Inner Stillness

Be glad of life because it gives you the chance to love and to work and to play and to look up at the stars.

HENRY VAN DYKE

I will be glad and rejoice in You; I will sing praise to Your name, O Most High.

Psalm 9:2, NKJV

NOW
is the TIME...

To See the Big Picture

*Worry weighs a person down; an encouraging
word cheers a person up.*

Proverbs 12:25, NLT

Sometimes it's so easy to get caught up in the details that
you forget there's a larger perspective. When you become
worried or negativity starts creeping in, that's a good sign
that it's time to step back and take a look at the big picture. An overwhelming problem gets reduced down to size
when you look at life from a higher perspective. Get a
God's-eye view of the situation. Meditate on eternal values, and see how your current situation looks in the light
of God's priorities.

*May he give you the desire of your heart
and make all your plans succeed.*

Psalm 20:4, NIV

*Aim at heaven and you get earth thrown in;
aim at earth and you get neither.*

C. S. LEWIS

NOW *is the* TIME...

To Picture Success

As he thinks in his heart, so is he.

Proverbs 23:7, NKJV

What is success to you? If you want authentic success, you need to think about what that really means to you. Imagine how it would feel to have the success you desire. What would your life look like? How would things be different? What would be the same? Now take one quality of the success you want to create, and start making it part of your life. For example, take a class to upgrade your skills in a particular area. Ask God to help you picture and create a success that honors Him.

I have it all planned out—plans to take care of you, not abandon you, plans to give you the future you hope for.

Jeremiah 29:11, THE MESSAGE

We can accomplish almost anything within our ability if we but think we can!

GEORGE MATTHEW ADAMS

NOW *is the* TIME...

To Pace Yourself

You enlarge my steps under me,
and my feet have not slipped.

Psalm 18:36, NAS

*E*asy does it. You don't have to do everything all at once.
Progress is made one step at a time. And those steps are
usually baby steps, not giant leaps! If you have a big job
ahead of you, focus on the immediate steps you can take
instead of allowing yourself to be overwhelmed by the
enormity of the task. This works in the spiritual life as
well. Growth in understanding comes one lesson at a
time. Be humble and gentle with yourself, choice by
choice, each day.

As God's chosen people, holy and dearly loved, clothe yourselves
with compassion, kindness, humility, gentleness and patience.

Colossians 3:12, NIV

By perseverance the snail reached the Ark.
CHARLES HADDON SPURGEON

NOW *is the* TIME...

To Live Sustainably

The godly are well rooted and bear their own fruit.
Proverbs 12:12, NLT

There are two ways to live sustainably. The first is to be conscious of how you use the resources of the earth, creating a simple lifestyle that is less wasteful and more ecologically sound. The second is to live mindfully, creating a life that is deeply rooted in your relationship to God. This kind of sustainability builds a house on the solid rock of inner simplicity, prayerfulness, and faith. You will live sustainably when you make life-enhancing choices that allow time for what is most important in life.

Man does not live by bread alone, but man lives by every word that comes from the mouth of the LORD.
Deuteronomy 8:3, ESV

Happiness consists more in small conveniences or pleasures that occur every day, than in great pieces of good fortune that happen but seldom.
BENJAMIN FRANKLIN

NOW
is the TIME...
To Let God Handle It

*The LORD is my rock and my fortress and my deliverer;
my God, my strength, in whom I will trust; my shield
and the horn of my salvation, my stronghold.*

Psalm 18:2, NKJV

When you've done your best and can do no more, let God handle it. When you don't know where to turn or what to do, let God take over. Let go of all you've been holding on to so tightly and put it in God's hands. This means you surrender your agenda and allow things to work themselves out. When you trust God as your source, miracles can happen. God is bigger than your biggest problem, stronger than your most frightening enemy, and greater than your most troublesome doubts and fears.

O LORD my God, in You I put my trust.

Psalm 7:1, NKJV

> *Only by trust in God can a man
> carrying responsibility find repose.*
> DWIGHT D. EISENHOWER

NOW *is the* TIME...

To Speak the Truth in Love

Speaking the truth in love, we are to grow up in every way into him who is the head, into Christ.

Ephesians 4:15, ESV

You can speak the truth and be destructive. Sometimes others are not ready to hear the truth, whether it's about the outfits they wear or the choices they make. Speaking the truth in love means that you temper your comments with kindness, seeking to serve others by meeting them where they are instead of where you think they should be. Speak the truth in love to yourself as well. Speak truths of God's love and forgiveness. Speak encouraging, kind words, and that will be the highest truth of all.

Speak the truth to each other.

Zechariah 8:16, NIV

We know the truth, not only by the reason, but also by the heart.

BLAISE PASCAL

NOW
is the TIME...
To Find Common Ground

*There is one body and one Spirit, just as also
you were called in one hope of your calling.*

Ephesians 4:4, NAS

*I*nstead of concentrating on the differences you have with others, look for common ground. The first place to look is in the heart of God. People who are different from you, with different opinions and different perspectives, are loved by God, as are you. That is an essential starting point. Then look at common human needs. Everyone needs to be loved, to feel safe and secure, and to have hopes and dreams honored. You do not have to agree with someone to find that you share common ground.

*Love one another. As I have loved you,
so you must love one another.*

John 13:34, NIV

God loves "otherness," but hell hates it.
CLYDE S. KILBY

NOW is the TIME...

To Walk Your Talk

The integrity of the honest keeps them on track;
the deviousness of crooks brings them to ruin.

Proverbs 11:3, THE MESSAGE

*I*ntegrity is a state of wholeness and congruency. The person of integrity does not say one thing and do another. As you progress in your spiritual life, you'll discover a growing sensitivity to a lack of integrity. You'll sense it in others when their work doesn't live up to their talk, but you'll also be more able to sense it in yourself. You'll know when there's a dissonance between what you say and what you do. It's a subtle spiritual skill and a sign of wholeness when you are wise enough to truly walk your talk.

A God-loyal life keeps you on track;
sin dumps the wicked in the ditch.

Proverbs 13:6, THE MESSAGE

Integrity is the first step to true greatness.
CHARLES SIMMONS

NOW
is the TIME...
To Challenge Your Assumptions

If you listen to constructive criticism, you will be at home among the wise. If you reject discipline, you only harm yourself; but if you listen to correction, you grow in understanding.

Proverbs 15:31–32, NLT

*A*re you willing to take a second look at some of your cherished assumptions? You can keep your comfortable opinions and beliefs, but you will pay a price for them. People used to assume the world was flat. They didn't like it when Galileo told them it was round. Just because you assume something is true doesn't mean it is. Have an open mind, and be willing to challenge comfortable assumptions. Though God's essential truths do not change, you need to change so you can grow in your understanding.

I pray that your love will overflow more and more, and that you will keep on growing in knowledge and understanding.

Philippians 1:9, NLT

He that never changes his opinions, never corrects his mistakes, will never be wiser on the morrow than he is today.

TRYON EDWARDS

NOW
is the TIME...

To Count Your Blessings

*Blessings will come upon you and accompany
you if you obey the LORD your God.*

Deuteronomy 28:2, NIV

*O*ne of the best antidotes to a case of the blues may be to count your blessings. A gloomy or negative view of life is often an unappreciative one, overlooking present goodness in search of some faraway desire or longing. Make a list of five things you are grateful for right now. You can start by thanking God for the gift of life. It sounds simplistic, but practicing daily appreciation and gratitude for life's blessings can make you aware that you are truly rich in the things that count.

*You serve me a six-course dinner right in front of my enemies.
You revive my drooping head; my cup brims with blessing.*

Psalm 23:5, THE MESSAGE

---

*The person who has stopped being
thankful has fallen asleep in life.*
ROBERT LOUIS STEVENSON

NOW *is the* TIME...

To Seek Divine Wisdom

To those called by God to salvation, both Jews and Gentiles,
Christ is the power of God and the wisdom of God.

1 Corinthians 1:24, NLT

*S*eeking God's wisdom can take many forms. You can study
and read scriptures or wise books. You can cultivate a regular
prayer time. You can also find wise counsel by talking with
others who are on the spiritual path. Do one more thing:
listen with your heart. Seek silence, quiet your mind, and
just be with God. You don't have to do anything. This is not
about performance, but about being present and waiting in
God's presence. You are attuning yourself to Him, so you
can understand His greatest wisdom.

A fool finds pleasure in evil conduct,
but a man of understanding delights in wisdom.

Proverbs 10:23, NIV

True wisdom is gazing at God. Gazing at
God is silence of the thoughts.
SAINT ISAAC THE SYRIAN

NOW
is the TIME...

To Care for Your Soul

*May God give you more and more grace and peace as you
grow in your knowledge of God and Jesus our Lord.*

2 Peter 1:2, NLT

A parish priest was often called a curate. His responsibility for tending the needs of his flock was known as *cura animarum*, the cure of souls. If you take this idea and apply it to yourself, you can imagine the responsibility you have to be the caretaker of your own soul. This can mean paying attention to the changes you go through on a daily basis. As you become an observer of the seasons of your soul, you begin to understand what it means to grow in God's grace.

*Keep sound wisdom and discretion; so they will
be life to your soul and grace to your neck.*

Proverbs 3:21–22, NKJV

*The human soul is God's treasury, out of
which he coins unspeakable riches.*

HENRY WARD BEECHER

NOW *is the* TIME...

To Give Up Perfectionism

If the Son makes you free,
you shall be free indeed.

John 8:36, NKJV

*P*eople are so hard on themselves. How often have you worked frenetically to build up an image of what you think you should be, only to feel like a failure because you fall short of your own vision of perfection? You think you are imperfect, incomplete, and broken. But God sees a gentler, wiser perfection. It is a perfection that loves the process and values the so-called flaws as part of a character in development. Give up unrealistic perfectionism so that you can live a real life free before God.

Christ has set us free to live a free life. So take your stand!
Never again let anyone put a harness of slavery on you.

Galatians 5:1, THE MESSAGE

Perfection is being, not doing; it is not to
effect an act but to achieve a character.

FULTON JOHN SHEEN

NOW *is the* TIME...

To Take a Sabbath

*I gave them my Sabbath days of rest as a sign between them
and me. It was to remind them that I am the LORD,
who had set them apart to be holy.*

Ezekiel 20:12, NLT

*R*emember the Sabbath" is not just a lifestyle suggestion
or a nice addition to the end of a busy week. A biblical day
of rest can be a revolutionary challenge to workaholism
and mindless accumulation of a society that never knows
when enough is enough. Taking a Sabbath—a sacred time
out—offers a way to listen to God, to reconnect with your
own soul, and to allow a period of rest and recuperation.
Remember to celebrate what is beautiful and eternal by
taking a Sabbath rest.

There remains a Sabbath rest for the people of God.

Hebrews 4:9, ESV

---

*Sabbath is a way of being in time where we remember who we are,
remember what we know, and taste the gifts of spirit and eternity.*

WAYNE MULLER

NOW
is the TIME...
To Listen to Your Body

*Glorify God in your body and in
your spirit, which are God's.*

1 Corinthians 6:20, NKJV

Your body is the sacred temple of God, woven in wonder and mystery in your mother's womb, and the humble bearer that carries you through your days. Often people treat the body as an enemy or stubborn donkey. But your body offers a deeper wisdom, from the sense of tired heaviness you feel in a negative situation to the gut feelings that tell you someone is not telling the whole truth. Learn to listen to the messages your body sends, for they are whispers of God's intelligence to guide you.

*Do you not know that your body is the temple of the
Holy Spirit... and you are not your own?*

1 Corinthians 6:19, NKJV

*Stress is the perception that we are
separate from our divine source.*
BRIAN LUKE SEAWARD

NOW
is the TIME...

To Find Your Balance

Rejoice not over me, O my enemy; when I fall, I shall rise;
when I sit in darkness, the LORD will be a light to me.

Micah 7:8, ESV

The dancer must learn to find balance in her art. The long-distance runner must balance the need for speed with the need for a sustainable pace that will take him to the finish line. When things are out of balance, the dancer falls and the runner falters. If you have felt unsteady on your feet lately, or have faltered in your ability to continue on, now is the time to regain your balance by reconnecting to God. Then you can maintain a healthy and happy balance in your life.

Those who hope in the LORD will renew their strength.
They will soar on wings like eagles; they will run and
not grow weary, they will walk and not be faint.

Isaiah 40:31, NIV

Moderation is the silken string running
though all the pearl chain of virtues.

JOSEPH HALL

NOW *is the* TIME...

To Appreciate the Differences

Everyone will recognize that you are my disciples—
when they see the love you have for each other.

John 13:35, THE MESSAGE

*A*s you seek to find common ground with others, you also
need to appreciate the differences instead of assuming that
differences are negative. If life is a banquet, there may be
many dishes that seem exotic and strange, but if you're
willing to try them, you might discover some new flavors
to enjoy. So it is with God's banquet of humanity. There
are many strange and exotic flavors of people, and it takes
a discerning person to appreciate the differences and
enjoy them. Life then becomes a feast, not a fight.

Beloved, let us love one another, for love is of God; and
everyone who loves is born of God and knows God. He
who does not love does not know God, for God is love.

1 John 4:7, NKJV

> *He alone loves the Creator perfectly who*
> *manifests a pure love for his neighbor.*
>
> VENERABLE BEDE

NOW
is the TIME...

To Be God's Ambassador

We are Christ's ambassadors; God is making his appeal through us. We speak for Christ when we plead, "Come back to God!"

2 Corinthians 5:20, NLT

When you are a part of God's kingdom, sometimes the old life feels like a foreign country. No longer do you judge by the standards of the world, because you now live, move, and have your spiritual being in another world. But you are still physically present, your old friends still know you, and you have a work to do while you're in this world. Be God's ambassador, treating others with love and respect. Be a reflection of God's love in this world, and love will reflect back to you.

He is not far from each one of us; for in Him we live and move and have our being.

Acts 17:27–28, NKJV

We are all pencils in the hand of a writing God, who is sending love letters to the world.

MOTHER TERESA

NOW *is the* TIME...

TO

Dream Big

•

Embrace Change

•

Step Out in Faith

•

Cultivate Inner Power

•

Trust Your Hunches

•

Know the Truth

•

Put Love into Action

•

Make Time for Fun

•

Appreciate the Differences

*Think big thoughts but
relish small pleasures.*

H. JACKSON BROWN JR.

*Yes, we should make the most of what God
gives, both the bounty and the capacity
to enjoy it, accepting what's given and
delighting in the work. It's God's gift!*

Ecclesiastes 5:19, THE MESSAGE

NOW *is the* TIME...

To Invite Inspiration

The earth is the LORD's, and everything in it,
the world, and all who live in it.

Psalm 24:1, NIV

*L*ike a breath of fresh air coming into a closed room, inspiration reminds you of your highest dreams and aspirations. It can be invited into your life by creating time and space for it. Who inspires you? Is there a hero, an author, or an artist who reminds you of your deepest potential? What inspires you? Walks in nature, the arts, worship? Invite inspiration by cultivating your gifts and doing something you love to do. Find inspiration in your relationship to God, and in the whisper of a quiet prayer.

It is He who made the earth by His power, who established
the world by His wisdom; and by His understanding
He has stretched out the heavens.

Jeremiah 10:12, NAS

Each of us has a fire in our heart for something.
It's our goal in life to find it and keep it lit.

MARY LOU RETTON

NOW
is the TIME...

To Practice the Presence

*You have kept my feet from slipping. So now I can walk
in your presence, O God, in your life-giving light.*

Psalm 56:13, NLT

God is here with you, right now, in this place. But if you
are too frazzled and distracted, you may miss experiencing
the sense of His presence. Instead of worrying about
tomorrow or regretting yesterday, focus on this moment.
Quiet your mind, and be attentive to God's presence here
and now. Practicing the presence of God can be done anywhere, but it is a learned skill. Beginning lessons start in
solitude and silence. Advanced lessons take place in a busy
kitchen or workshop. God's presence is with you wherever
you are.

*Let the godly rejoice. Let them be glad in God's
presence. Let them be filled with joy.*

Psalm 68:3, NLT

---

*There is no place where the Presence of God is not, only people
who are not fully present in the places where they are.*

KEN CAREY

NOW *is the* TIME...

To Treasure This Moment

You mark us with blessing, O God, our God.
Psalm 67:6, THE MESSAGE

*T*reasure this moment today. Tomorrow is still a dream and yesterday a memory. Like a river that flows without stopping, time flows on moment by moment. When you learn to treasure the moment with gratitude, you will drink the fullness of the time God has allotted you. Be present with God in this moment, pausing to thank Him for what is around you right now. Then really take the time to pay attention to your life—the sights and scents and sounds and impressions. These are God's gift to you.

The Father wants to give you the very kingdom itself.
Luke 12:32, THE MESSAGE

> *God, the master of time, never gives the future.*
> *He gives only the present, moment by moment.*
> THE CLOUD OF UNKNOWING

NOW *is the* TIME...

To Work Playfully

The humble will see their God at work and be glad.

Psalm 69:32, NLT

Are you worried about your workload? Are you so serious about what you are doing that you've drained the creativity and joy out of it? It's time to bring a more playful attitude to earning your daily bread and a more creative approach to whatever work you do. Instead of seeing your work as an overwhelming task, think of it as a playful project. Use your creativity to imagine alternative solutions, and set aside concerns about what others will think. Concentrate on doing a wonderful job, and trust God with the results.

You will eat the fruit of your labor;
blessings and prosperity will be yours.

Psalm 128:2, NIV

The future is as bright as the promises of God.
ADONIRAM JUDSON

NOW *is the* TIME...

To Cultivate Confidence

Is not your fear of God your confidence,
and the integrity of your ways your hope?

Job 4:6, ESV

*S*omewhere along the way, some people are taught that it
is conceited to be confident. So their lives are spent being
diffident wallflowers instead of plunging into the dance of
life. But confidence is a virtue to be cultivated, not a vice
to be avoided. You are unique, and God called you to offer
your gifts to the world. But those gifts will never be given
if you don't cultivate a calm confidence and belief in yourself. Cultivate confidence by taking God's opinion of your
potential and possibilities more seriously.

The effect of righteousness will be peace, and the result
of righteousness, quietness and trust forever.

Isaiah 32:17, ESV

Faith is a living, daring confidence in God's grace.
MARTIN LUTHER

NOW is the TIME...

To Find Strength in Vulnerability

He remembered us in our weakness.
His faithful love endures forever.

Psalm 136:23, NLT

*D*o you think of being vulnerable as godlike? Most people don't. They're afraid of vulnerability, thinking it's a sign of weakness. But in God's kingdom, vulnerability is a sign of strength. Vulnerability partakes of the very nature of God, who is not afraid to set aside all His power and glory to become a part of humanity. In the Christ child born in the Christmas stable and the crucified and risen Christ of Easter, you see a picture of God's vulnerability. Humanity's definition of weakness is God's definition of strength.

I am glad to boast about my weaknesses, so that
the power of Christ can work through me.

2 Corinthians 12:9, NLT

To love at all is to be vulnerable. The only place outside Heaven where you can be perfectly safe from all the dangers of love is—Hell.

C. S. LEWIS

NOW
is the TIME...

To Work Wholeheartedly

Be strong and courageous, and do the work.
1 Chronicles 28:20, NLT

*W*ork is a gift from God. It is the natural expression of your abilities, the thing in which you can find mental, physical, and spiritual satisfaction. When you work wholeheartedly at a task, you forget yourself. Completely absorbed in the task at hand, you lose track of time and plunge into the pleasure of accomplishing good or making the world a better place. Whether your work is making beds and doing dishes or running a business, put your heart into your work, and work will be its own reward.

A man will be satisfied with good by the fruit of his words,
and the deeds of a man's hands will return to him.

Proverbs 12:14, NAS

Hard work is a thrill and a joy when you are in the will of God.
ROBERT A. COOK

NOW
is the TIME...

To Attempt Great Things

*Hazael responded, "How could a nobody like
me ever accomplish such great things?"*

2 Kings 8:13, NLT

*W*hat one thing would you do if you were brave enough
to attempt it? Do you cherish a yet-unfulfilled dream in
your heart? Do you think you are too small to attempt
making that dream come true? Then think again. It's not
just you alone, all by yourself. It's you and God together.
God is your partner in the co-creation of any dream. You
can move mountains with a little bit of faith and the willingness to put forth a great deal of effort. With the grace
of God, anything is possible.

*May he give you the power to accomplish all
the good things your faith prompts you to do.*

2 Thessalonians 1:11, NLT

> *What great thing would you attempt
> if you knew you could not fail?*
> ROBERT SCHULLER

NOW *is the* TIME...

To Do What's Right for You

All this comes from the God who settled the relationship between us and him, and then called us to settle our relationships with each other.

2 Corinthians 5:18, THE MESSAGE

When you were a child, you loved what you loved and never wondered whether it was worth loving. But as you grew older, peer pressure often made you want to fit in with the crowd and like what you thought other people wanted you to like. But God has a better idea. He created you as a unique person with gifts, talents, and interests like no one else's. Trust Him more deeply by believing that doing what's right for you will help you fulfill God's intentions for your life.

Be generous with the different things God gave you, passing them around so all get in on it.

1 Peter 4:10, THE MESSAGE

> *You must be holy in the way God asks you to be holy.*
> *God does not ask you to be a Trappist monk or a hermit.*
> *He wills that you sanctify your everyday life.*
> SAINT VINCENT PALLOTTI

NOW
is the TIME...

To Let Go of the Past

There is no remembrance of men of old,
and even those who are yet to come will
not be remembered by those who follow.

Ecclesiastes 1:11, NIV

*I*f you're holding on to the past, you're carrying dead
weight. You cannot bring the good things of the past back,
and you cannot right the wrongs of yesterday by denying
today. You can treasure the memories and trust God's forgiveness. Clinging to the past is counterproductive. Put
the past into the hands of God so you can live today fully.
Ask forgiveness for past wrongs, and forgive others for
what they did to you. Start today anew by trusting God.
All times are in His hands, but you have only today.

He seldom reflects on the days of his life, because God
keeps him occupied with gladness of heart.

Ecclesiastes 5:20, NIV

Life can only be understood backwards,
but it must be lived forwards.
SØREN KIERKEGAARD

NOW *is the* TIME...

To Be Truly Free

Deal courageously, and may the LORD be with the upright!
2 Chronicles 19:11, ESV

*I*t takes courage to live as a free human being. If you would be truly free, then you need a courageous heart. Courage isn't thoughtless bravado in the face of danger. It's a deep trust, knowing that even when you are most frightened, God will give—and has already given—all the resources you need to face the situation and meet the need. Whether you need the courage to face a difficult situation or to acknowledge a difficult truth or just want the courage to face the day with faith, now is the time for courage. God will be with you.

March on, my soul, with might!
Judges 5:21, ESV

> *Courage is being scared to death—and saddling up anyway.*
> JOHN WAYNE

NOW *is the* TIME...

To Read a Good Book

Listen to the words of the wise;
apply your heart to my instruction.

Proverbs 22:17, NLT

*W*alk into any library or bookstore, and you will find a treasure trove of inspiration, entertainment, and wisdom. Books enrich lives, and never more so than when you are led to exactly the right book at the right time. If you want to enlarge your mind and expand your experience, read a good book. It might be a spiritual classic, a novel that introduces you to intriguing characters, or a compendium of information on a compelling subject. Make books your regular companions. They will offer wisdom and insight for life's pilgrimage.

Love wisdom like a sister; make insight
a beloved member of your family.

Proverbs 7:4, NLT

Reading is to the mind what exercise is to the body.
JOSEPH ADDISON

NOW
is the TIME...

To Cultivate Contentment

*Godliness actually is a means of great gain
when accompanied by contentment.*

1 Timothy 6:6, NAS

*C*ontentment is an attitude, and it can be a way of life. In a never-enough world of buying and selling, choosing to be contented with what you have is a radical decision. By appreciating the riches you already have, you calm the all-too-human urge of wanting more. Turn it into gratitude to God instead. Look around you right now and see what treasures of contentment lie close at hand. Appreciate a cozy home, good friendships, loving families, and peaceful communities. Contentment makes you feel wealthy.

I have learned to be content in whatever circumstances I am.

Philippians 4:11, NAS

---

*There are times when a man should be content
with what he has, but never with what he is.*

WILLIAM GEORGE JORDAN

NOW *is the* TIME...

To Keep a Clear Conscience

Create in me a pure heart, O God,
and renew a steadfast spirit within me.

Psalm 51:10, NIV

*L*isten to your conscience. It is God's voice in your heart, guiding you to do the right thing. Keeping a clear conscience brings you a sense of inner peace by connecting you to God's grace. If you have made choices you regret, ask forgiveness and, if possible, make restitution. The more you listen to the guidance of your conscience, the more sensitive and accurate it will be. Then you will steer clear of dangerous temptations and debilitating guilt. And you will live a happier and more peaceful life.

My righteousness I hold fast, and will not let it go;
my heart shall not reproach me as long as I live.

Job 27:6, NKJV

Labor to keep alive in your breast that little
spark of celestial fire called conscience.

GEORGE WASHINGTON

NOW *is the* TIME...

To Value Humility

Fear-of-GOD is a school in skilled living—
first you learn humility, then you experience glory.

Proverbs 15:33, THE MESSAGE

*H*umility is vastly underrated in an advertising-oriented
society. Being humble is a positive virtue, freeing you to
live a life of purpose and service. A humble person has no
need to defend his reputation or to sell others on what he
is accomplishing. His actions and his presence say all that
needs saying. When you value humility, you are free to be
open to listening to God and learning from others. You
will no longer waste energy defending ego and pride. You
can experience greatness in your life by being humble.

The payoff for meekness and Fear-of-GOD is
plenty and honor and a satisfying life.

Proverbs 22:4, THE MESSAGE

A humble man can do great things with an uncommon
perfection because he is no longer concerned about accidentals,
like his own interests, and his own reputation.

THOMAS MERTON

NOW
is the TIME...

To Rule Your Mind

*All this I tested by wisdom and I said,
"I am determined to be wise."*

Ecclesiastes 7:23, NIV

*W*hat you think about God, about yourself, about others, and about how life works makes a great deal of difference in your daily life. Your thoughts are the starting point of your actions. If you think negative or limiting thoughts, you will make choices that lead to a more limited life. If you think expansive thoughts of faith and trust, you'll find that a richer, more expansive life follows. You can train your mind to think in more positive ways. Thoughts are the building blocks of your experience. Build well.

*May all my thoughts be pleasing to him,
for I rejoice in the LORD.*

Psalm 104:34, NLT

Wisdom is knowledge, rightly applied.

AUTHOR UNKNOWN

NOW
is the TIME...

To Give Anonymously

You will be enriched in every way to be generous in every way.
2 Corinthians 9:11, ESV

*I*t's a lot of fun to give an anonymous gift. First of all, you need to decide who the recipient will be and what you want to give him. Then there's the fun of devising clever ways to get the gift into his hands. How can you get your gift to someone without revealing your own identity? After the gift is given, there's a certain warmth around the heart, knowing that you were collaborating with God to bring a blessing to someone else. It's a secret between you and God. Your satisfaction comes from knowing your heart was focused on the other person and not on yourself.

*Good works are conspicuous, and even those
that are not cannot remain hidden.*

1 Timothy 5:25, ESV

> *You do not have to be rich to be generous. If he has the spirit
> of true generosity, a pauper can give like a prince.*
> CORRINE U. WELLS

NOW *is the* TIME...

To Pray in All Situations

*As soon as I pray, you answer me; you
encourage me by giving me strength.*

Psalm 138:3, NLT

*P*rayer is more than making a request or begging for mercy. Prayer is a collaboration with God, a way of paying attention to the sacred in everyday life. God is present in every situation. Wherever you are, He is there. Cultivate a greater awareness of God's presence in your life through prayer. Prayer can be an active sense of fellowship with God. Bring your concerns, give thanks and praise, and rest in God's presence through meditation and contemplation. You'll enjoy an ongoing conversation with Him in all situations.

*I am praying to you because I know you will answer,
O God. Bend down and listen as I pray.*

Psalm 17:6, NLT

---

*Prayer is not merely an occasional impulse to which we respond
when we are in trouble; prayer is a life attitude.*

WALTER A. MUELLER

NOW
is the **TIME...**

TO

Treasure This Moment

·

Attempt Great Things

·

Trust in All Seasons

·

Create Positive Change

·

Depend on God

·

Be Patient

·

Eliminate Nonessentials

·

Remain Faithful

·

Give Anonymously

Everybody can be great. Because anybody can serve. . . . You only need a heart full of grace. A soul generated by love.

MARTIN LUTHER KING

The greatest among you should be like the youngest, and the one who rules like the one who serves.

Luke 22:26, NIV

NOW *is the* TIME...

To Eliminate Nonessentials

*If you wish to be complete, go and sell your possessions and give
to the poor, and you will have treasure in heaven.*

Matthew 19:21, NAS

*F*ocus on what's really essential. Ask yourself these questions: Do I consider the activities I engage in to be worthwhile? Would I choose to do this if I didn't feel obligated to do it? Is my reason for doing this worthy? Will what I am doing have a positive impact? If I had only six months to live, would I do anything different with the time in my day? If many of the activities you engage in seem superfluous or onerous, it's time to look at what is most important to you. Ask for God's guidance to help you eliminate the nonessentials.

*Consider the lilies, how they grow: they neither toil nor spin;
but I tell you, not even Solomon in all his glory
clothed himself like one of these.*

Luke 12:27, NAS

---

*Purity and simplicity are the two wings with
which man soars above the earth and all temporary nature.*

THOMAS À KEMPIS

NOW
is the TIME...

To Expect the Unexpected

*The foolishness of God is wiser than men,
and the weakness of God is stronger than men.*

1 Corinthians 1:25, NKJV

God has a better idea, so seek His wisdom. While people plan and visualize from the limited perspective of human understanding and experience, God sees the larger picture. Life is complex and mysterious, so trusting in divine timing and celestial planning is essential. In a life that's lived from a spiritual understanding, you learn to expect the unexpected. God works in mysterious ways, His wonders to perform. Expect that divine timing will put you in touch with the right person at the right time—delightfully and unexpectedly.

*Many, O LORD my God, are Your wonderful works which
You have done; and Your thoughts toward us cannot be
recounted to You in order; if I would declare and speak
of them, they are more than can be numbered.*

Psalm 40:5, NKJV

*One never knows what each day is going to bring.
The important thing is to be open and ready for it.*

HENRY MOORE

NOW
is the TIME...

To Trust in All Seasons

I've already run for dear life straight to the arms of GOD.
Psalm 11:1, THE MESSAGE

*L*ife has its seasons. If you have felt the chill of winter in your bones, and if all your hopes and dreams seem to have dried up and blown away, keep trusting. Even when it's winter in your soul, the divine wisdom of God is still at work. The Creator of the earth and its seasons also controls the tempo of the seasons in your life. As you learn to trust God in the difficult times, so you will reap the rewards of that quiet trust as spring appears again.

Blessed be GOD—he heard me praying. He proved he's on my side; I've thrown my lot in with him. Now I'm jumping for joy, and shouting and singing my thanks to him.

Psalm 28:6-7, THE MESSAGE

> *Our Lord has written the promise of resurrection,*
> *not in books alone, but in every leaf in springtime.*
> MARTIN LUTHER

NOW
is the TIME...

To Be Patient

May you be strengthened with all power, according to his glorious might, for all endurance and patience with joy.

Colossians 1:11, ESV

As you wait for spring to return and God's timing to unfold in your life, treasure the gift of patience. This is not patience with a martyrlike sigh of complaint. This is an active, faith-filled, patient trust in the goodness of God, the wisdom of life itself, and the knowledge that all good things take time to come to fruition. Focus on the task today, trusting God with tomorrow. Patience is a fruit of the Spirit, and its wise cultivation will result in a rich harvest of blessings.

Afterward you may go and celebrate because of all the good things the LORD your God has given to you and your household.

Deuteronomy 26:11, NLT

Patience is a bitter plant, but it has sweet fruit.
GERMAN PROVERB

NOW
is the TIME...

To Be Productive

*Honor the LORD with your wealth and
with the firstfruits of all your produce.*

Proverbs 3:9, ESV

*F*ocus on the task at hand. Put your best effort out right
now, and do it energetically with a good attitude. Make
productive use of your time and energy. If you see something that needs to be done, do it. If you have a dream you
want to see come true, work on it and pray for wisdom.
Is there a practical step you can take? Then take it. These
are all attitudes that enhance your productivity. But even
more than that, ask yourself if it's something worth doing.

*We ask God to give you complete knowledge of his will and to
give you spiritual wisdom and understanding. Then the way
you live will always honor and please the Lord, and
your lives will produce every kind of good fruit.*

Colossians 1:9–10, NLT

Men will get no more out of life than they put into it.
WILLIAM J. H. BOETCKER

NOW
is the TIME...

To Be Hopeful

Having hope will give you courage.
You will be protected and will rest in safety.

Job 11:18, NLT

When you hope, you are showing your trust that God will work the situation out for good. Hope offers a spiritual grace to calm your fears and keep the divine fire of faith lit in your heart. When you are tempted to be sad or cynical, make a different choice. Choose a deeper trust in God, and focus on the hope in a situation or for a person. By choosing to live in hope and to think positively about the potential outcome, you are making a statement of faith in God. God is the author of and reason for hope.

May integrity and honesty protect me,
for I put my hope in you.

Psalm 25:21, NLT

When you say a situation or a person is hopeless,
you are slamming a door in the face of God.
CHARLES L. ALLEN

NOW
is the TIME...

To Look for Role Models

*Josiah ... did right in the sight of the LORD,
and walked in the ways of his father David.*

2 Chronicles 34:1-2, NAS

*P*ositive role models help you see what is possible. So look
for encouragement and inspiration in the lives of others.
You can begin with books. There are heroic and inspiring
stories waiting on the library or bookstore shelf, stories
both past and present. Look also for role models in the
people around you. Most people do not consider themselves heroic, yet if you learn about their stories of survival
and grace, you discover that they can teach you how to
lead a life of deep and abiding faith.

*Ezekiel will be a sign to you; according
to all that he has done you will do.*

Ezekiel 24:24, NAS

---

*He is truly great who is little in his own
eyes and makes nothing of the highest honor.*

THOMAS À KEMPIS

NOW
is the TIME...

To Be Progressive

Oh, that my steps might be steady,
keeping to the course you set.
Psalm 119:5, THE MESSAGE

*P*rogressive isn't a political party or believing in the power of progress. Being progressive is the opposite of being regressive. When you are progressive, you are open to new ideas and new ways of doing things. You are flexible and willing to change. You are eager to learn and realize that God has many ways of bringing good to you. To be progressive in the very best sense is to be willing to release old ideas, thoughts, and ways of living that no longer serve your highest good.

Meditate on these things; give yourself entirely to them,
that your progress may be evident to all.
1 Timothy 4:15, NKJV

Only in growth, reform, and change, paradoxically
enough, is true security to be found.
ANNE MORROW LINDBERGH

NOW
is the TIME...

To Create Positive Change

*B*e the change you want to see in the world. If you don't
like the way things are, take responsibility to contribute to
the solution instead of complaining and staying stuck in
the problem. Since change is inevitable, the choice isn't
between changing or not changing; rather, the choice is
between choosing how you will change and why. Instead of
dragging your feet, be practical and proactive. Make change
your ally instead of your enemy. Ask God for wisdom and
guidance to help you navigate the currents of change.

---

*Christians are supposed not merely to endure change,
nor even to profit by it, but to cause it.*

HARRY EMERSON FOSDICK

NOW *is the* TIME...

To Trust Your Finer Instincts

Discretion will protect you,
and understanding will guard you.

Proverbs 2:11, NIV

*I*f you hear gossip about someone you know, but you believe this person is innocent of the slander, trust that instinct. When there is a choice between two good options, choose the option that your heart tells you is right. As you grow in the spiritual life and become more attuned to the ways of God, you'll discover a greater sensitivity to right and wrong. You'll also have a more nuanced sense of authentic value. When you have a choice between better and best, trust your finer instincts.

Blessed are they who maintain justice,
who constantly do what is right.

Psalm 106:3, NIV

It is only by following your deepest instinct
that you can lead a rich life.
KATHARINE BUTLER HATHAWAY

NOW
is the TIME...

To Enjoy Life

*Everyone also to whom God has given wealth and possessions
and power to enjoy them, and to accept his lot and
rejoice in his toil—this is the gift of God.*

Ecclesiastes 5:19, ESV

*T*his is your one precious life. Do not squander it in anger,
criticism, and self-absorption. Enjoying life as a child included
tasting its wonders and being open to new experiences, and as
adults it's often necessary to learn to again enjoy life as a
child would. As you are exchanging toxic thoughts and
habits for life-sustaining ideas and actions, ask God to bring
a fresh understanding of how beautiful and precious your
one earthly life is. Then offer thanks to God by enjoying the
gift He has bestowed on you—life itself.

*Reach out and experience the breadth! Test its
length! Plumb the depths! Rise to the heights!
Live full lives, full in the fullness of God.*

Ephesians 3:18–19, THE MESSAGE

---

*I sincerely believe we are given life to enjoy and make it more enjoyable
for others. The best way to do this is to get in the middle of it.*

HENRY L. HARREL SR.

NOW
is the TIME...
To Keep Learning

*Listen, friends, to some fatherly advice; sit up and take
notice so you'll know how to live. I'm giviing you good
counsel; don't let it go in one ear and out the other.*

Proverbs 4:1–2, THE MESSAGE

*G*od gave you a mind to think, as well as the sense and
sensibility to learn and absorb new information and fresh
ideas. And then He placed you in a world of wonder and
infinite possibilities. Adopt an attitude of openness and
commit yourself to lifelong learning. Always be ready to
dive into new subjects, to listen to and learn from fascinating
people, and to explore the world with the eagerness of a
child. It's not a matter of learning all the answers, but
learning to ask the important questions.

Let the Spirit renew your thoughts and attitudes.

Ephesians 4:23, NLT

---

*We have an infinite amount to learn both
from nature and from each other.*
JOHN GLENN

NOW
is the TIME...
To Recognize Opportunity

Don't miss a trick. Make the most of every opportunity.
Colossians 4:5, THE MESSAGE

*E*very day brings its opportunities. There is always an opportunity to learn something new or appreciate something familiar. And then there are the days when a divine appointment drops a life-changing opportunity into your lap. It may be a small beginning, but for those who have attuned their hearts to see God's grace at work in all things, the opportunity is recognized, welcomed, and appreciated. And because you have cultivated your spiritual understanding, you'll have the understanding to recognize a golden opportunity when it arrives.

While we have opportunity, let us do good to all people, and especially to those who are of the household of the faith.
Galatians 6:10, NAS

God's best gift to us is not things, but opportunities.
ALICE W. ROLLINS

NOW
is the TIME...

To Be Cheerful

The light of the eyes rejoices the heart.
Proverbs 15:30, NKJV

*G*ood cheer and happiness are not the same things. Happiness is felt when outer circumstances conspire to bring you what you desire. Cheerfulness is an attitude and a choice. It's a decision to make the most of whatever comes to you, and to do this in ways that lift everybody's spirits. This kind of attitude grows from a mature faith that understands life may have its difficulties, but you don't have to make it more difficult with a rotten attitude. Don't let difficulties get the best of you. When you are tempted to complain, choose cheer instead.

Your comforts delight my soul.
Psalm 94:19, NKJV

---

*Cheerfulness, like spring, opens all
the blossoms of the inward man.*
JEAN PAUL RICHTER

NOW *is the* TIME...

To Seek Wise Counsel

*About face! I can revise your life. Look, I'm ready to pour
out my spirit on you; I'm ready to tell you all I know.*

Proverbs 1:23, THE MESSAGE

*I*f you are surrounded by yes-men who are always telling you
how wonderful you are, how right you are, and how wise
you are—you are in *big* trouble. Jesus talked about the
blind leading the blind, steering straight for a ditch. What
you really need is wise counsel from someone who will
help you see a different perspective and who will tell you
the difficult truths you may not want to hear. Ask God to
guide you to wise counsel—and to give you the wisdom to
appreciate it.

*Dear friend, pay close attention to this, my wisdom;
listen very closely to the way I see it.*

Proverbs 5:1, THE MESSAGE

---

*Hope for the best, get ready for the worst,
and then take what God chooses to send.*

MATTHEW HENRY

NOW *is the* TIME...

To Refrain from Anger

A fool gives full vent to his anger, but a wise
man keeps himself under control.

Proverbs 29:11, NIV

*A*nger is fueled by a habitual way of looking at the world. Anger can be a pattern of behavior, a choice of thoughts, and an attitude toward life. Ask yourself what triggers your anger. You'll probably find the person or circumstance that sets you off is different every time, but the pattern of your behavior is always the same. Instead of nursing anger in your heart, ask God to show you how to transform your urge to become angry into a passion for inner peace and gentle patience.

Do not be quickly provoked in your spirit,
for anger resides in the lap of fools.

Ecclesiastes 7:9, NIV

Anger is quieted by a gentle word just
as fire is quenched by water.

SAINT FRANCIS DE SALES

NOW
is the TIME...
To Be an Encourager

The lips of the righteous feed many.
Proverbs 10:21, ESV

*E*verybody is a critic these days. Experts abound in criticism, grading and comparing and eager to tell others where they need to improve. Encouragement is even more necessary in times like these. Look for the good in others—and in yourself—and encourage that instead of finding fault. Encouragement is like a helping hand. Most people underestimate their own abilities, and a bit of well-spoken appreciation can remind them of their God-given gifts and talents. By being an encourager, you'll bring a healing touch of God's love to life.

If your gift is to encourage others, be encouraging.
Romans 12:8, NLT

> *Encouragement costs you nothing to give,*
> *but it is priceless to receive.*
> AUTHOR UNKNOWN

NOW *is the* TIME...

To Depend on God

The LORD is good to those who depend on him,
to those who search for him.

Lamentations 3:25, NLT

*L*ife is larger than you are. And so in the complexities and perplexities of living, learn to depend on God for wisdom, help, and comfort. Your dependence is not about being needy or childish; it's about being empowered to take personal responsibility for your life, knowing that God is always for you, never against you. Therefore, you can dare to live life fully and with the consequences of your choices, because your choices, in the end, have grown out of the wisdom of depending on God.

Come back to your God. Act with love
and justice, and always depend on him.

Hosea 12:6, NLT

The more we depend on God the more
dependable we find he is.

CLIFF RICHARD

NOW *is the* TIME...

TO

Enjoy Life

·

Reach for the Stars

·

Affirm Your Faith

·

Let Go of the Past

·

Be an Encourager

·

Live in Peace

·

Think Long Term

·

Cultivate Contentment

·

Expect the Unexpected

Knowledge is love and light and vision.
HELEN KELLER

*The heart of him who has
understanding seeks knowledge.*

Proverbs 15:14, NKJV

NOW *is the* TIME...

To Live in Peace

O man greatly loved, fear not, peace be
with you; be strong and of good courage.

Daniel 10:19, ESV

*I*nner peace is a skill as much as it is an attitude or experience. It is honed over time by the choices you make, whether choosing to refrain from anger or taking time every day to seek inner calm in the presence of God. Let the peace of God rule in your heart, and make choices that create peace in your life. Promote peace by the way you treat others, too. Treat the people you meet or work with as if they were your brothers or sisters. Treat them with honor and respect and love. By choosing to live in peace, you will become a peacemaker who enjoys the special blessing of God.

Strive for peace with everyone.

Hebrews 12:14, ESV

If the basis of peace is God, the secret of peace is trust.

J. B. FIGGIS

NOW
is the TIME...

To Remain Faithful

You must continue in the things which you have learned and been assured of, knowing from whom you have learned them.

2 Timothy 3:14, NKJV

When everyone around you is unfaithful, remain faithful. When you face choices between right and wrong, be faithful by making right choices. Faithfulness is keeping your commitments, honoring your promises, and following through on your intentions. Live out a positive faith in all situations. And when you are weary and tempted to toss it all aside in times of discouragement, ask God to help you remain faithful. He will give you the courage and energy to keep on keeping on, and remain faithful to your highest ideals.

We have become partakers of Christ if we hold the beginning of our confidence steadfast to the end.

Hebrews 3:14, NKJV

God did not call us to be successful, but to be faithful.
MOTHER TERESA

NOW
is the TIME...

To Be Bold

With that kind of hope to excite us, nothing holds us back.
2 Corinthians 3:12, THE MESSAGE

*H*ave you been hesitating, longing to commit to a dream, but afraid it will never come true? Have you been timid, holding back when you wanted to speak up, shy when you wanted to be bold? Remind yourself that God is with you and within you. Rest in the strength and assurance of God's changeless character. Let that be the basis of your boldness and freedom of expression. For then you can be bolder and braver than any lion, standing up for what you believe in and who you are.

Honest people are relaxed and confident, bold as lions.
Proverbs 28:1, THE MESSAGE

Even a mouse can squeak with boldness when
he stands on the shoulders of an elephant.
DUDLEY ADAMS

NOW *is the* TIME...

To Be Pure in Heart

Blessed are the pure in heart, for they will see God.
Matthew 5:8, NIV

*C*hristianity offers an understanding that innocence once lost can be found again, and that being renewed by a baptism of love covers a multitude of sins. While you cannot change your past choices, you can begin today by choosing to cultivate a purity of heart that comes from the depths of God's love and forgiveness. By paying attention to the motivations of your heart, and choosing the highest good for all in everything you do, you can be pure in heart and intention from now on.

Rejoice in the LORD and be glad, you righteous;
sing, all you who are upright in heart!
Psalm 32:11, NIV

How to be pure? By steadfast longing
for the one good, that is, God.
MEISTER ECKEHART

NOW *is the* TIME...

To Reach for the Stars

I press on toward the goal.
Philippians 3:14, ESV

*D*are to believe that God is with you and wants you to
reach for your deepest dreams and highest ideals. Nothing
is impossible with God, so nothing is impossible to those
who trust in God. Never underestimate the potential of
the partnership between you and God. He planted the life
force within you, and just as a seed pushes through the soil
and reaches for its sunlit destiny, so you are born to reach
for the stars. Eternity is in your heart, so trust in that and
aim high.

*We always pray for you, that our God may make you
worthy of his calling and may fulfill every resolve for
good and every work of faith by his power.*

2 Thessalonians 1:11, ESV

*Ideals are like the stars—we never reach them, but like
the mariners of the sea we chart our course by them.*
CARL SCHURZ